Blue Ocean Strategy
Complete Self-Assessment

The guidance in this Self-Assessment is based on Blue Ocean Strategy best practices and standards in business process architecture, design and quality management. The guidance is also based on the professional judgment of the individual collaborators listed in the Acknowledgments.

Notice of rights

You are licensed to use the Self-Assessment contents in your presentations and materials for internal use and customers without asking us - we are here to help.

All rights reserved for the book itself: this book may not be reproduced or transmitted in any form by any means, electronic, mechanical, photocopying, recording, or otherwise, without the prior written permission of the publisher.

The information in this book is distributed on an "As Is" basis without warranty. While every precaution has been taken in the preparation of he book, neither the author nor the publisher shall have any liability to any person or entity with respect to any loss or damage caused or alleged to be caused directly or indirectly by the instructions contained in this book or by the products described in it.

Trademarks

Many of the designations used by manufacturers and sellers to distinguish their products are claimed as trademarks. Where those designations appear in this book, and the publisher was aware of a trademark claim, the designations appear as requested by the owner of the trademark. All other product names and services identified throughout this book are used in editorial fashion only and for the benefit of such companies with no intention of infringement of the trademark. No such use, or the use of any trade name, is intended to convey endorsement or other affiliation with this book.

Copyright © by The Art of Service
http://theartofservice.com
service@theartofservice.com

Table of Contents

About The Art of Service	7
Acknowledgments	8
Included Resources - how to access	9
Your feedback is invaluable to us	11
Purpose of this Self-Assessment	11
How to use the Self-Assessment	12
Blue Ocean Strategy Scorecard Example	14
Blue Ocean Strategy Scorecard	15
BEGINNING OF THE SELF-ASSESSMENT:	16
CRITERION #1: RECOGNIZE	17
CRITERION #2: DEFINE:	27
CRITERION #3: MEASURE:	41
CRITERION #4: ANALYZE:	56
CRITERION #5: IMPROVE:	67
CRITERION #6: CONTROL:	77
CRITERION #7: SUSTAIN:	87
Blue Ocean Strategy and Managing Projects, Criteria for Project Managers:	130
1.0 Initiating Process Group: Blue Ocean Strategy	131
1.1 Project Charter: Blue Ocean Strategy	133
1.2 Stakeholder Register: Blue Ocean Strategy	135

1.3 Stakeholder Analysis Matrix: Blue Ocean Strategy   136

2.0 Planning Process Group: Blue Ocean Strategy   138

2.1 Project Management Plan: Blue Ocean Strategy   140

2.2 Scope Management Plan: Blue Ocean Strategy   142

2.3 Requirements Management Plan: Blue Ocean Strategy   144

2.4 Requirements Documentation: Blue Ocean Strategy   146

2.5 Requirements Traceability Matrix: Blue Ocean Strategy   148

2.6 Project Scope Statement: Blue Ocean Strategy   150

2.7 Assumption and Constraint Log: Blue Ocean Strategy   152

2.8 Work Breakdown Structure: Blue Ocean Strategy   154

2.9 WBS Dictionary: Blue Ocean Strategy   156

2.10 Schedule Management Plan: Blue Ocean Strategy   159

2.11 Activity List: Blue Ocean Strategy   161

2.12 Activity Attributes: Blue Ocean Strategy   163

2.13 Milestone List: Blue Ocean Strategy   165

2.14 Network Diagram: Blue Ocean Strategy   167

2.15 Activity Resource Requirements: Blue Ocean Strategy   169

2.16 Resource Breakdown Structure: Blue Ocean Strategy 170

2.17 Activity Duration Estimates: Blue Ocean Strategy 172

2.18 Duration Estimating Worksheet: Blue Ocean Strategy 174

2.19 Project Schedule: Blue Ocean Strategy 176

2.20 Cost Management Plan: Blue Ocean Strategy 178

2.21 Activity Cost Estimates: Blue Ocean Strategy 180

2.22 Cost Estimating Worksheet: Blue Ocean Strategy 182

2.23 Cost Baseline: Blue Ocean Strategy 184

2.24 Quality Management Plan: Blue Ocean Strategy 186

2.25 Quality Metrics: Blue Ocean Strategy 188

2.26 Process Improvement Plan: Blue Ocean Strategy 190

2.27 Responsibility Assignment Matrix: Blue Ocean Strategy 192

2.28 Roles and Responsibilities: Blue Ocean Strategy 194

2.29 Human Resource Management Plan: Blue Ocean Strategy 196

2.30 Communications Management Plan: Blue Ocean Strategy 198

2.31 Risk Management Plan: Blue Ocean Strategy 200

2.32 Risk Register: Blue Ocean Strategy 202

2.33 Probability and Impact Assessment: Blue Ocean Strategy 204

2.34 Probability and Impact Matrix: Blue Ocean Strategy 206

2.35 Risk Data Sheet: Blue Ocean Strategy 208

2.36 Procurement Management Plan: Blue Ocean Strategy 210

2.37 Source Selection Criteria: Blue Ocean Strategy 212

2.38 Stakeholder Management Plan: Blue Ocean Strategy 214

2.39 Change Management Plan: Blue Ocean Strategy 216

3.0 Executing Process Group: Blue Ocean Strategy 218

3.1 Team Member Status Report: Blue Ocean Strategy 220

3.2 Change Request: Blue Ocean Strategy 222

3.3 Change Log: Blue Ocean Strategy 224

3.4 Decision Log: Blue Ocean Strategy 226

3.5 Quality Audit: Blue Ocean Strategy 228

3.6 Team Directory: Blue Ocean Strategy 231

3.7 Team Operating Agreement: Blue Ocean Strategy 233

3.8 Team Performance Assessment: Blue Ocean Strategy 235

3.9 Team Member Performance Assessment: Blue Ocean Strategy 237

3.10 Issue Log: Blue Ocean Strategy   239

4.0 Monitoring and Controlling Process Group: Blue Ocean
Strategy   241

4.1 Project Performance Report: Blue Ocean Strategy   243

4.2 Variance Analysis: Blue Ocean Strategy   245

4.3 Earned Value Status: Blue Ocean Strategy   247

4.4 Risk Audit: Blue Ocean Strategy   249

4.5 Contractor Status Report: Blue Ocean Strategy   251

4.6 Formal Acceptance: Blue Ocean Strategy   253

5.0 Closing Process Group: Blue Ocean Strategy   255

5.1 Procurement Audit: Blue Ocean Strategy   257

5.2 Contract Close-Out: Blue Ocean Strategy   259

5.3 Project or Phase Close-Out: Blue Ocean Strategy   261

5.4 Lessons Learned: Blue Ocean Strategy   263
Index   266

About The Art of Service

The Art of Service, Business Process Architects since 2000, is dedicated to helping stakeholders achieve excellence.

Defining, designing, creating, and implementing a process to solve a stakeholders challenge or meet an objective is the most valuable role… In EVERY group, company, organization and department.

Unless you're talking a one-time, single-use project, there should be a process. Whether that process is managed and implemented by humans, AI, or a combination of the two, it needs to be designed by someone with a complex enough perspective to ask the right questions.

Someone capable of asking the right questions and step back and say, 'What are we really trying to accomplish here? And is there a different way to look at it?'

With The Art of Service's Standard Requirements Self-Assessments, we empower people who can do just that — whether their title is marketer, entrepreneur, manager, salesperson, consultant, Business Process Manager, executive assistant, IT Manager, CIO etc... —they are the people who rule the future. They are people who watch the process as it happens, and ask the right questions to make the process work better.

Contact us when you need any support with this Self-Assessment and any help with templates, blue-prints and examples of standard documents you might need:

http://theartofservice.com
service@theartofservice.com

Acknowledgments

This checklist was developed under the auspices of The Art of Service, chaired by Gerardus Blokdyk.

Representatives from several client companies participated in the preparation of this Self-Assessment.

In addition, we are thankful for the design and printing services provided.

Included Resources - how to access

Included with your purchase of the book is the Blue Ocean Strategy Self-Assessment Spreadsheet Dashboard which contains all questions and Self-Assessment areas and auto-generates insights, graphs, and project RACI planning - all with examples to get you started right away.

How? Simply send an email to
access@theartofservice.com
with this books' title in the subject to get the Blue Ocean Strategy Self Assessment Tool right away.

You will receive the following contents with New and Updated specific criteria:

- The latest quick edition of the book in PDF

- The latest complete edition of the book in PDF, which criteria correspond to the criteria in...

- The Self-Assessment Excel Dashboard, and...

- Example pre filled Self Assessment Excel Dashboard to get familiar with results generation

- In-depth specific Checklists covering the topic

- Project management checklists and templates to assist with implementation

INCLUDES LIFETIME SELF ASSESSMENT UPDATES

Every self assessment comes with Lifetime Updates and Lifetime Free Updated Books. Lifetime Updates is an industry-first feature which allows you to receive verified self assessment updates, ensuring you always have the most accurate information at your fingertips.

Get it now- you will be glad you did - do it now, before you forget.

Send an email to **access@theartofservice.com** with this books' title in the subject to get the Blue Ocean Strategy Self Assessment Tool right away.

Your feedback is invaluable to us

If you recently bought this book, we would love to hear from you! You can do this by writing a review on amazon (or the online store where you purchased this book) about your last purchase! As part of our continual service improvement process, we love to hear real client experiences and feedback.

How does it work?
To post a review on Amazon, just log in to your account and click on the Create Your Own Review button (under Customer Reviews) of the relevant product page. You can find examples of product reviews in Amazon. If you purchased from another online store, simply follow their procedures.

What happens when I submit my review?
Once you have submitted your review, send us an email at review@theartofservice.com with the link to your review so we can properly thank you for your feedback.

Purpose of this Self-Assessment

This Self-Assessment has been developed to improve understanding of the requirements and elements of Blue Ocean Strategy, based on best practices and standards in business process architecture, design and quality management.

It is designed to allow for a rapid Self-Assessment to determine how closely existing management practices and procedures correspond to the elements of the Self-Assessment.

The criteria of requirements and elements of Blue Ocean Strategy have been rephrased in the format of a Self-Assessment questionnaire, with a seven-criterion scoring system, as explained in this document.

In this format, even with limited background knowledge of Blue

Ocean Strategy, a manager can quickly review existing operations to determine how they measure up to the standards. This in turn can serve as the starting point of a 'gap analysis' to identify management tools or system elements that might usefully be implemented in the organization to help improve overall performance.

How to use the Self-Assessment

On the following pages are a series of questions to identify to what extent your Blue Ocean Strategy initiative is complete in comparison to the requirements set in standards.

To facilitate answering the questions, there is a space in front of each question to enter a score on a scale of '1' to '5'.

> 1 Strongly Disagree
>
> 2 Disagree
>
> 3 Neutral
>
> 4 Agree
>
> 5 Strongly Agree

Read the question and rate it with the following in front of mind:

**'In my belief,
the answer to this question is clearly defined'.**

There are two ways in which you can choose to interpret this statement;
1. how aware are you that the answer to the question is clearly defined
2. for more in-depth analysis you can choose to gather

evidence and confirm the answer to the question. This obviously will take more time, most Self-Assessment users opt for the first way to interpret the question and dig deeper later on based on the outcome of the overall Self-Assessment.

A score of '1' would mean that the answer is not clear at all, where a '5' would mean the answer is crystal clear and defined. Leave emtpy when the question is not applicable or you don't want to answer it, you can skip it without affecting your score. Write your score in the space provided.

After you have responded to all the appropriate statements in each section, compute your average score for that section, using the formula provided, and round to the nearest tenth. Then transfer to the corresponding spoke in the Blue Ocean Strategy Scorecard on the second next page of the Self-Assessment.

Your completed Blue Ocean Strategy Scorecard will give you a clear presentation of which Blue Ocean Strategy areas need attention.

Blue Ocean Strategy Scorecard Example

Example of how the finalized Scorecard can look like:

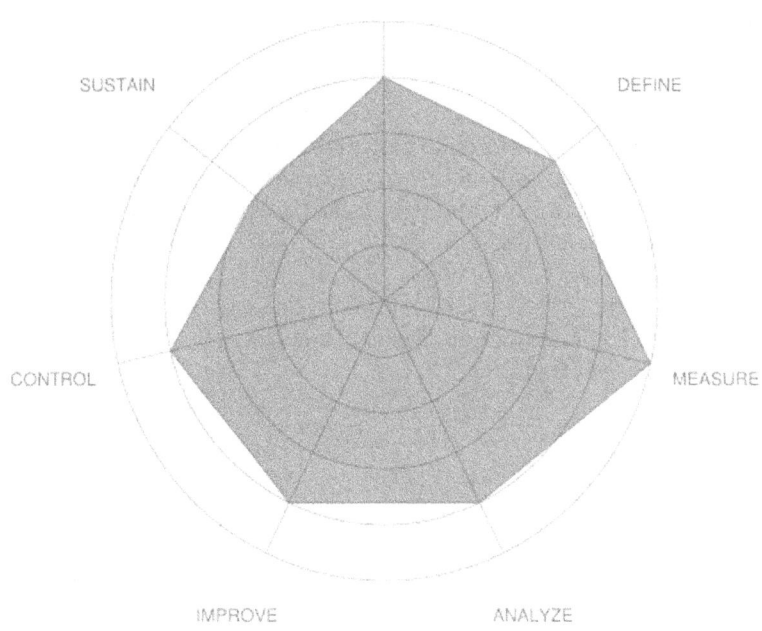

Blue Ocean Strategy Scorecard

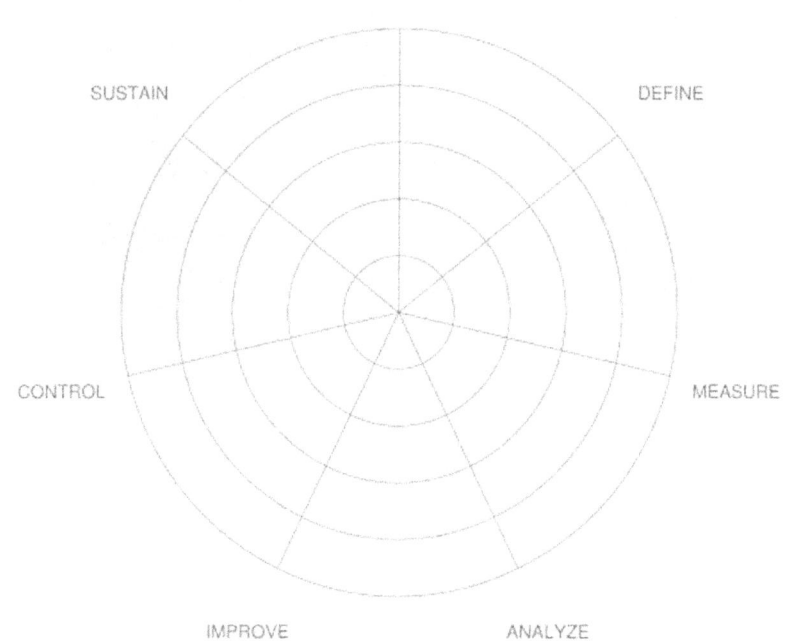

BEGINNING OF THE SELF-ASSESSMENT:

CRITERION #1: RECOGNIZE

INTENT: Be aware of the need for change. Recognize that there is an unfavorable variation, problem or symptom.

In my belief, the answer to this question is clearly defined:

5 Strongly Agree

4 Agree

3 Neutral

2 Disagree

1 Strongly Disagree

1. What problems are you facing and how do you consider Blue Ocean Strategy will circumvent those obstacles?
<--- Score

2. What customer problem does it solve?
<--- Score

3. What tools and technologies are needed for a

custom Blue Ocean Strategy project?
<--- Score

4. Is the need for organizational change recognized?
<--- Score

5. What do you need to adapt?
<--- Score

6. Is there a strategic group that you need to take account of?
<--- Score

7. Is there a legal or environmental issue of the product disposal?
<--- Score

8. Will Blue Ocean Strategy deliverables need to be tested and, if so, by whom?
<--- Score

9. Are you dealing with any of the same issues today as yesterday? What can you do about this?
<--- Score

10. When a Blue Ocean Strategy manager recognizes a problem, what options are available?
<--- Score

11. What alternatives and key issues did your team consider?
<--- Score

12. What do you need to start doing?
<--- Score

13. What should be considered when identifying available resources, constraints, and deadlines?
<--- Score

14. How long does it take to find the product you need?
<--- Score

15. Are controls defined to recognize and contain problems?
<--- Score

16. What would happen if Blue Ocean Strategy weren't done?
<--- Score

17. How are the Blue Ocean Strategy's objectives aligned to the group's overall stakeholder strategy?
<--- Score

18. Do you need other products and services to make your product work?
<--- Score

19. Is a lot of capital needed to enter your industry?
<--- Score

20. How does it fit into your organizational needs and tasks?
<--- Score

21. Who needs what information?
<--- Score

22. What needs to be aligned in strategy

implementation and execution?
<--- Score

23. What do you need to get?
<--- Score

24. Does the team have all the information and tools it needs?
<--- Score

25. Does the buyer need a lot of important information?
<--- Score

26. How long to find the product you need?
<--- Score

27. Are employees recognized or rewarded for performance that demonstrates the highest levels of integrity?
<--- Score

28. What are the key issues you face in your business?
<--- Score

29. How are you going to measure success?
<--- Score

30. Are your goals realistic? Do you need to redefine your problem? Perhaps the problem has changed or maybe you have reached your goal and need to set a new one?
<--- Score

31. Are problem definition and motivation clearly

presented?
<--- Score

32. To what extent does each concerned units management team recognize Blue Ocean Strategy as an effective investment?
<--- Score

33. Are there any specific expectations or concerns about the Blue Ocean Strategy team, Blue Ocean Strategy itself?
<--- Score

34. Which customer (unmet) needs are you satisfying ?
<--- Score

35. What is the smallest subset of the problem you can usefully solve?
<--- Score

36. Do you need different information or graphics?
<--- Score

37. What else needs to be measured?
<--- Score

38. What vendors make products that address the Blue Ocean Strategy needs?
<--- Score

39. How much money do you think you need?
<--- Score

40. What resources do you need to implement your strategy?

<--- Score

41. Will a response program recognize when a crisis occurs and provide some level of response?
<--- Score

42. How do you take a forward-looking perspective in identifying Blue Ocean Strategy research related to market response and models?
<--- Score

43. What prevents you from making the changes you know will make you a more effective Blue Ocean Strategy leader?
<--- Score

44. What training and capacity building actions are needed to implement proposed reforms?
<--- Score

45. As a sponsor, customer or management, how important is it to meet goals, objectives?
<--- Score

46. What activities does the governance board need to consider?
<--- Score

47. What issues are being talked about in your community?
<--- Score

48. What are your needs in relation to Blue Ocean Strategy skills, labor, equipment, and markets?
<--- Score

49. How do you define a problem?
<--- Score

50. Does Blue Ocean Strategy create potential expectations in other areas that need to be recognized and considered?
<--- Score

51. Have you identified your Blue Ocean Strategy key performance indicators?
<--- Score

52. To what extent would your organization benefit from being recognized as a award recipient?
<--- Score

53. What is the context in which your product or service is issued?
<--- Score

54. What information do users need?
<--- Score

55. What is the problem or issue?
<--- Score

56. What issue is most important to your organization right now?
<--- Score

57. What are the issues involved in new entrants into the industry?
<--- Score

58. What are the stakeholder objectives to be achieved with Blue Ocean Strategy?

<--- Score

59. Which information does the Blue Ocean Strategy business case need to include?
<--- Score

60. What situation(s) led to this Blue Ocean Strategy Self Assessment?
<--- Score

61. What does Blue Ocean Strategy success mean to the stakeholders?
<--- Score

62. What are the expected benefits of Blue Ocean Strategy to the stakeholder?
<--- Score

63. Do you need a strategy or strategic innovation?
<--- Score

64. Will new equipment/products be required to facilitate Blue Ocean Strategy delivery, for example is new software needed?
<--- Score

65. What is the problem you are trying to solve?
<--- Score

66. Is your communication tool appropriate for your topic, issue and message?
<--- Score

67. Does your organization need more Blue Ocean Strategy education?
<--- Score

68. Who needs to know about Blue Ocean Strategy?
<--- Score

69. Who else hopes to benefit from it?
<--- Score

70. What do you need?
<--- Score

71. Are there any revenue recognition issues?
<--- Score

72. Think about the people you identified for your Blue Ocean Strategy project and the project responsibilities you would assign to them. what kind of training do you think they would need to perform these responsibilities effectively?
<--- Score

73. How do you identify the kinds of information that you will need?
<--- Score

74. How much are sponsors, customers, partners, stakeholders involved in Blue Ocean Strategy? In other words, what are the risks, if Blue Ocean Strategy does not deliver successfully?
<--- Score

75. Do you know what you need to know about Blue Ocean Strategy?
<--- Score

Add up total points for this section:
_ _ _ _ _ = Total points for this section

Divided by: _____ (number of statements answered) = _____
Average score for this section

Transfer your score to the Blue Ocean Strategy Index at the beginning of the Self-Assessment.

CRITERION #2: DEFINE:

INTENT: Formulate the stakeholder problem. Define the problem, needs and objectives.

In my belief, the answer to this question is clearly defined:

5 Strongly Agree

4 Agree

3 Neutral

2 Disagree

1 Strongly Disagree

1. Are your organizations challenges clearly defined?
<--- Score

2. Is a fully trained team formed, supported, and committed to work on the Blue Ocean Strategy improvements?
<--- Score

3. What is the context in which your product or service is used?

<--- Score

4. Are stakeholder processes mapped?

<--- Score

5. What key stakeholder process output measure(s) does Blue Ocean Strategy leverage and how?

<--- Score

6. Has your scope been defined?

<--- Score

7. Is there a completed SIPOC representation, describing the Suppliers, Inputs, Process, Outputs, and Customers?

<--- Score

8. How do you manage unclear Blue Ocean Strategy requirements?

<--- Score

9. What are the Blue Ocean Strategy use cases?

<--- Score

10. How do you define Key Success Factors for different industry segments ?

<--- Score

11. Where can you gather more information?

<--- Score

12. Who are the Blue Ocean Strategy improvement team members, including Management Leads and Coaches?

<--- Score

13. Is Blue Ocean Strategy currently on schedule according to the plan?
<--- Score

14. Has the direction changed at all during the course of Blue Ocean Strategy? If so, when did it change and why?
<--- Score

15. What constraints exist that might impact the team?
<--- Score

16. How do you gather requirements?
<--- Score

17. Is the team adequately staffed with the desired cross-functionality? If not, what additional resources are available to the team?
<--- Score

18. What specifically is the problem? Where does it occur? When does it occur? What is its extent?
<--- Score

19. Is the Blue Ocean Strategy scope manageable?
<--- Score

20. What are the compelling stakeholder reasons for embarking on Blue Ocean Strategy?
<--- Score

21. What are the requirements for success in this industry?

<--- Score

22. Have the customer needs been translated into specific, measurable requirements? How?
<--- Score

23. Has a project plan, Gantt chart, or similar been developed/completed?
<--- Score

24. When are meeting minutes sent out? Who is on the distribution list?
<--- Score

25. Is the team sponsored by a champion or stakeholder leader?
<--- Score

26. Has the improvement team collected the 'voice of the customer' (obtained feedback – qualitative and quantitative)?
<--- Score

27. What critical content must be communicated – who, what, when, where, and how?
<--- Score

28. Do the problem and goal statements meet the SMART criteria (specific, measurable, attainable, relevant, and time-bound)?
<--- Score

29. How do you keep key subject matter experts in the loop?
<--- Score

30. Is data collected and displayed to better understand customer(s) critical needs and requirements.
<--- Score

31. Why are you doing Blue Ocean Strategy and what is the scope?
<--- Score

32. Is there a Blue Ocean Strategy management charter, including stakeholder case, problem and goal statements, scope, milestones, roles and responsibilities, communication plan?
<--- Score

33. How is the team tracking and documenting its work?
<--- Score

34. Are there any constraints known that bear on the ability to perform Blue Ocean Strategy work? How is the team addressing them?
<--- Score

35. Is full participation by members in regularly held team meetings guaranteed?
<--- Score

36. When is/was the Blue Ocean Strategy start date?
<--- Score

37. Do you have a Blue Ocean Strategy success story or case study ready to tell and share?
<--- Score

38. Are customers identified and high impact areas

defined?
<--- Score

39. Has a Blue Ocean Strategy requirement not been met?
<--- Score

40. How does the Blue Ocean Strategy manager ensure against scope creep?
<--- Score

41. What is the worst case scenario?
<--- Score

42. What customer feedback methods were used to solicit their input?
<--- Score

43. Is the team equipped with available and reliable resources?
<--- Score

44. Is the team formed and are team leaders (Coaches and Management Leads) assigned?
<--- Score

45. Are there clearly defined activities in place to overcome organization challenges?
<--- Score

46. Has everyone on the team, including the team leaders, been properly trained?
<--- Score

47. What is in the scope and what is not in scope?
<--- Score

48. How do you catch Blue Ocean Strategy definition inconsistencies?
<--- Score

49. How and when will the baselines be defined?
<--- Score

50. How do you define innovation in your organization?
<--- Score

51. How was the 'as is' process map developed, reviewed, verified and validated?
<--- Score

52. Does the scope remain the same?
<--- Score

53. What defines best in class?
<--- Score

54. Is Blue Ocean Strategy linked to key stakeholder goals and objectives?
<--- Score

55. What are the Roles and Responsibilities for each team member and its leadership? Where is this documented?
<--- Score

56. Are customer(s) identified and segmented according to their different needs and requirements?
<--- Score

57. Has the Blue Ocean Strategy work been fairly and/

or equitably divided and delegated among team members who are qualified and capable to perform the work? Has everyone contributed?
<--- Score

58. Is the improvement team aware of the different versions of a process: what they think it is vs. what it actually is vs. what it should be vs. what it could be?
<--- Score

59. How do you gather the stories?
<--- Score

60. How would you define Blue Ocean Strategy leadership?
<--- Score

61. What system do you use for gathering Blue Ocean Strategy information?
<--- Score

62. What sort of initial information to gather?
<--- Score

63. How have you defined all Blue Ocean Strategy requirements first?
<--- Score

64. What qualities do you feel define great leadership?
<--- Score

65. Are improvement team members fully trained on Blue Ocean Strategy?
<--- Score

66. Are resources adequate for the scope?
<--- Score

67. What is the scope of Blue Ocean Strategy?
<--- Score

68. What are the dynamics of the communication plan?
<--- Score

69. Is there a completed, verified, and validated high-level 'as is' (not 'should be' or 'could be') stakeholder process map?
<--- Score

70. Has/have the customer(s) been identified?
<--- Score

71. Will team members regularly document their Blue Ocean Strategy work?
<--- Score

72. How do you hand over Blue Ocean Strategy context?
<--- Score

73. Is the current 'as is' process being followed? If not, what are the discrepancies?
<--- Score

74. Is there a critical path to deliver Blue Ocean Strategy results?
<--- Score

75. What happens if Blue Ocean Strategy's scope changes?

<--- Score

76. What are the record-keeping requirements of Blue Ocean Strategy activities?
<--- Score

77. Are team charters developed?
<--- Score

78. What scope to assess?
<--- Score

79. Has a high-level 'as is' process map been completed, verified and validated?
<--- Score

80. How do you think the partners involved in Blue Ocean Strategy would have defined success?
<--- Score

81. Are accountability and ownership for Blue Ocean Strategy clearly defined?
<--- Score

82. Has anyone else (internal or external to the group) attempted to solve this problem or a similar one before? If so, what knowledge can be leveraged from these previous efforts?
<--- Score

83. Does the product require external maintenance?
<--- Score

84. When is the estimated completion date?
<--- Score

85. How did the Blue Ocean Strategy manager receive input to the development of a Blue Ocean Strategy improvement plan and the estimated completion dates/times of each activity?
<--- Score

86. How will variation in the actual durations of each activity be dealt with to ensure that the expected Blue Ocean Strategy results are met?
<--- Score

87. What are your organizational enablers required for the strategy?
<--- Score

88. Is the scope of Blue Ocean Strategy defined?
<--- Score

89. Are required metrics defined, what are they?
<--- Score

90. Have specific policy objectives been defined?
<--- Score

91. What was the context?
<--- Score

92. Is special Blue Ocean Strategy user knowledge required?
<--- Score

93. How will the Blue Ocean Strategy team and the group measure complete success of Blue Ocean Strategy?
<--- Score

94. What scope do you want your strategy to cover?
<--- Score

95. How are consistent Blue Ocean Strategy definitions important?
<--- Score

96. Is scope creep really all bad news?
<--- Score

97. Are different versions of process maps needed to account for the different types of inputs?
<--- Score

98. Are there different segments of customers?
<--- Score

99. How often are the team meetings?
<--- Score

100. If substitutes have been appointed, have they been briefed on the Blue Ocean Strategy goals and received regular communications as to the progress to date?
<--- Score

101. How do you manage changes in Blue Ocean Strategy requirements?
<--- Score

102. What baselines are required to be defined and managed?
<--- Score

103. What is the scope of the Blue Ocean Strategy

effort?
<--- Score

104. Is there regularly 100% attendance at the team meetings? If not, have appointed substitutes attended to preserve cross-functionality and full representation?
<--- Score

105. Does the product require training or expert assistance?
<--- Score

106. Will team members perform Blue Ocean Strategy work when assigned and in a timely fashion?
<--- Score

107. Scope of sensitive information?
<--- Score

108. Does the team have regular meetings?
<--- Score

109. What would be the goal or target for a Blue Ocean Strategy's improvement team?
<--- Score

110. What are the rough order estimates on cost savings/opportunities that Blue Ocean Strategy brings?
<--- Score

111. What are the boundaries of the scope? What is in bounds and what is not? What is the start point? What is the stop point?
<--- Score

112. Has a team charter been developed and communicated?
<--- Score

113. What information do you gather?
<--- Score

Add up total points for this section:
_ _ _ _ _ = Total points for this section

Divided by: _ _ _ _ _ _ (number of statements answered) = _ _ _ _ _ _
Average score for this section

Transfer your score to the Blue Ocean Strategy Index at the beginning of the Self-Assessment.

CRITERION #3: MEASURE:

INTENT: Gather the correct data. Measure the current performance and evolution of the situation.

In my belief, the answer to this question is clearly defined:

5 Strongly Agree

4 Agree

3 Neutral

2 Disagree

1 Strongly Disagree

1. Have you found any 'ground fruit' or 'low-hanging fruit' for immediate remedies to the gap in performance?
<--- Score

2. Do you have any cost Blue Ocean Strategy limitation requirements?
<--- Score

3. How do you do risk analysis of rare, cascading, catastrophic events?
<--- Score

4. What relevant entities could be measured?
<--- Score

5. Do the benefits outweigh the costs?
<--- Score

6. Among the Blue Ocean Strategy product and service cost to be estimated, which is considered hardest to estimate?
<--- Score

7. Are indirect costs charged to the Blue Ocean Strategy program?
<--- Score

8. How much does it cost?
<--- Score

9. Is key measure data collection planned and executed, process variation displayed and communicated and performance baselined?
<--- Score

10. What causes investor action?
<--- Score

11. What is the right balance of time and resources between investigation, analysis, and discussion and dissemination?
<--- Score

12. Is data collected on key measures that were

identified?
<--- Score

13. Have the concerns of stakeholders to help identify and define potential barriers been obtained and analyzed?
<--- Score

14. What are you verifying?
<--- Score

15. Does Blue Ocean Strategy systematically track and analyze outcomes for accountability and quality improvement?
<--- Score

16. How do you focus on what is right -not who is right?
<--- Score

17. Does Blue Ocean Strategy analysis show the relationships among important Blue Ocean Strategy factors?
<--- Score

18. Are the units of measure consistent?
<--- Score

19. Which measures and indicators matter?
<--- Score

20. What does your operating model cost?
<--- Score

21. What are the estimated costs of proposed changes?

<--- Score

22. Which stakeholder characteristics are analyzed?
<--- Score

23. Do you focus on a particular market niche?
<--- Score

24. What particular quality tools did the team find helpful in establishing measurements?
<--- Score

25. What kind of analytics data will be gathered?
<--- Score

26. What are your thoughts on the three ocean litter priority strategies?
<--- Score

27. Who should receive measurement reports?
<--- Score

28. What are your customers expectations and measures?
<--- Score

29. Does the Blue Ocean Strategy task fit the client's priorities?
<--- Score

30. Are actual costs in line with budgeted costs?
<--- Score

31. How can you reduce the costs of obtaining inputs?
<--- Score

32. When are costs are incurred?
<--- Score

33. Is the cost worth the Blue Ocean Strategy effort ?
<--- Score

34. What data was collected (past, present, future/ongoing)?
<--- Score

35. How are measurements made?
<--- Score

36. What could cause you to change course?
<--- Score

37. Can you do Blue Ocean Strategy without complex (expensive) analysis?
<--- Score

38. Are you able to realize any cost savings?
<--- Score

39. How do you measure lifecycle phases?
<--- Score

40. How will costs be allocated?
<--- Score

41. Does the customer face any significant costs in switching suppliers?
<--- Score

42. When is a best-cost provider strategy appealing?
<--- Score

43. How frequently do you verify your Blue Ocean Strategy strategy?
<--- Score

44. How can you measure the performance?
<--- Score

45. How do you identify and analyze stakeholders and their interests?
<--- Score

46. How do you know that any Blue Ocean Strategy analysis is complete and comprehensive?
<--- Score

47. Which costs should be taken into account?
<--- Score

48. What are the costs and benefits?
<--- Score

49. What are the agreed upon definitions of the high impact areas, defect(s), unit(s), and opportunities that will figure into the process capability metrics?
<--- Score

50. What happens if cost savings do not materialize?
<--- Score

51. How will effects be measured?
<--- Score

52. Do your customers incur any significant costs in switching suppliers?
<--- Score

53. What are the costs of delaying Blue Ocean Strategy action?
<--- Score

54. How can you reduce costs?
<--- Score

55. What potential environmental factors impact the Blue Ocean Strategy effort?
<--- Score

56. What measurements are being captured?
<--- Score

57. Will it be possible to measure any changes afterwards?
<--- Score

58. What metrics measure your organization success?
<--- Score

59. Are high impact defects defined and identified in the stakeholder process?
<--- Score

60. What are the costs and benefits of action in both qualitative and quantitative terms?
<--- Score

61. What are the current costs of the Blue Ocean Strategy process?
<--- Score

62. Are the Blue Ocean Strategy benefits worth its

costs?
<--- Score

63. Is long term and short term variability accounted for?
<--- Score

64. What key measures identified indicate the performance of the stakeholder process?
<--- Score

65. When a disaster occurs, who gets priority?
<--- Score

66. The approach of traditional Blue Ocean Strategy works for detail complexity but is focused on a systematic approach rather than an understanding of the nature of systems themselves, what approach will permit your organization to deal with the kind of unpredictable emergent behaviors that dynamic complexity can introduce?
<--- Score

67. What are the operational costs after Blue Ocean Strategy deployment?
<--- Score

68. How do you verify the authenticity of the data and information used?
<--- Score

69. What are the uncertainties surrounding estimates of impact?
<--- Score

70. How do you aggregate measures across priorities?

<--- Score

71. How does the rise in social media impact your Blue Ocean Strategy?
<--- Score

72. Do you have enough information to support or verify a conclusion?
<--- Score

73. Is a solid data collection plan established that includes measurement systems analysis?
<--- Score

74. Is data collection planned and executed?
<--- Score

75. Does your strategy focus on a problem in a new way?
<--- Score

76. Are process variation components displayed/ communicated using suitable charts, graphs, plots?
<--- Score

77. What circumstances would have an extreme impact on your organization?
<--- Score

78. Are supply costs steady or fluctuating?
<--- Score

79. What is a quantified Value Proposition ?
<--- Score

80. What are your primary costs, revenues, assets?

<--- Score

81. Does it have focus?
<--- Score

82. Does Blue Ocean Strategy analysis isolate the fundamental causes of problems?
<--- Score

83. What would be a real cause for concern?
<--- Score

84. Is there an opportunity to verify requirements?
<--- Score

85. Do you aggressively reward and promote the people who have the biggest impact on creating excellent Blue Ocean Strategy services/products?
<--- Score

86. Was a life-cycle cost analysis performed?
<--- Score

87. How do you verify Blue Ocean Strategy completeness and accuracy?
<--- Score

88. How can you measure Blue Ocean Strategy in a systematic way?
<--- Score

89. At what cost?
<--- Score

90. What methods are feasible and acceptable to estimate the impact of reforms?

<--- Score

91. Where are the cost savings?
<--- Score

92. How large is the gap between current performance and the customer-specified (goal) performance?
<--- Score

93. What does verifying compliance entail?
<--- Score

94. What is the total cost related to deploying Blue Ocean Strategy, including any consulting or professional services?
<--- Score

95. What is your Blue Ocean Strategy quality cost segregation study?
<--- Score

96. Who participated in the data collection for measurements?
<--- Score

97. Why do you expend time and effort to implement measurement, for whom?
<--- Score

98. What causes extra work or rework?
<--- Score

99. What drives O&M cost?
<--- Score

100. Are losses documented, analyzed, and remedial processes developed to prevent future losses?
<--- Score

101. Who is involved in verifying compliance?
<--- Score

102. Is Process Variation Displayed/Communicated?
<--- Score

103. What charts has the team used to display the components of variation in the process?
<--- Score

104. Have changes been properly/adequately analyzed for effect?
<--- Score

105. What is the impact of age on brand choice?
<--- Score

106. What could cause delays in the schedule?
<--- Score

107. How do you measure variability?
<--- Score

108. How can a Blue Ocean Strategy test verify your ideas or assumptions?
<--- Score

109. Have design-to-cost goals been established?
<--- Score

110. Which buyer group does your industry typically focus on?

<--- Score

111. How should the brand team measure its success?

<--- Score

112. Are you taking your company in the direction of better and revenue or cheaper and cost?

<--- Score

113. What determines if your organization is cost competitive?

<--- Score

114. Can you measure the return on analysis?

<--- Score

115. How will success or failure be measured?

<--- Score

116. Was a data collection plan established?

<--- Score

117. Is there a Performance Baseline?

<--- Score

118. Have the types of risks that may impact Blue Ocean Strategy been identified and analyzed?

<--- Score

119. How is the value delivered by Blue Ocean Strategy being measured?

<--- Score

120. Does a Blue Ocean Strategy quantification method exist?

<--- Score

121. How do you stay flexible and focused to recognize larger Blue Ocean Strategy results?
<--- Score

122. What has the team done to assure the stability and accuracy of the measurement process?
<--- Score

123. Has a cost center been established?
<--- Score

124. What are the most important costs of your business model?
<--- Score

125. What are the key input variables? What are the key process variables? What are the key output variables?
<--- Score

126. How do you verify and develop ideas and innovations?
<--- Score

127. What circumstances would have a disastrous impact on your organization?
<--- Score

128. Which objective will have the most impact on key decision makers and stakeholders?
<--- Score

129. Are key measures identified and agreed upon?
<--- Score

130. Which objective could cause the most negative impact if it is not completed?
<--- Score

131. How will measures be used to manage and adapt?
<--- Score

132. Do you effectively measure and reward individual and team performance?
<--- Score

Add up total points for this section:
_____ = Total points for this section

Divided by: _____ (number of statements answered) = _____
Average score for this section

Transfer your score to the Blue Ocean Strategy Index at the beginning of the Self-Assessment.

CRITERION #4: ANALYZE:

INTENT: Analyze causes, assumptions and hypotheses.

In my belief, the answer to this question is clearly defined:

5 Strongly Agree

4 Agree

3 Neutral

2 Disagree

1 Strongly Disagree

1. Are your outputs consistent?
<--- Score

2. Do your contracts/agreements contain data security obligations?
<--- Score

3. Were Pareto charts (or similar) used to portray the 'heavy hitters' (or key sources of variation)?
<--- Score

4. What controls do you have in place to protect data?
<--- Score

5. How do you gather data on customers?
<--- Score

6. What are your current levels and trends in key Blue Ocean Strategy measures or indicators of product and process performance that are important to and directly serve your customers?
<--- Score

7. Do you see a process of deinstrustrialization happening?
<--- Score

8. How do your work systems and key work processes relate to and capitalize on your core competencies?
<--- Score

9. How was the detailed process map generated, verified, and validated?
<--- Score

10. What are the disruptive Blue Ocean Strategy technologies that enable your organization to radically change your business processes?
<--- Score

11. What were the financial benefits resulting from any 'ground fruit or low-hanging fruit' (quick fixes)?
<--- Score

12. Are there decision roles, process, and time frame to be respected?

<--- Score

13. What qualifications are necessary?
<--- Score

14. Are gaps between current performance and the goal performance identified?
<--- Score

15. Is the final output clearly identified?
<--- Score

16. What is the cost of poor quality as supported by the team's analysis?
<--- Score

17. What are your Blue Ocean Strategy processes?
<--- Score

18. Can process help your business to succeed?
<--- Score

19. Does the outlook for the industry offer an attractive opportunity?
<--- Score

20. Who gets your output?
<--- Score

21. When will the strategy be implemented and related data collected?
<--- Score

22. What are evaluation criteria for the output?
<--- Score

23. What other organizational variables, such as reward systems or communication systems, affect the performance of this Blue Ocean Strategy process?
<--- Score

24. Identify an operational issue in your organization, for example, could a particular task be done more quickly or more efficiently by Blue Ocean Strategy?
<--- Score

25. Who qualifies to gain access to data?
<--- Score

26. What data do you need to collect?
<--- Score

27. Was a detailed process map created to amplify critical steps of the 'as is' stakeholder process?
<--- Score

28. What are your current levels and trends in key measures or indicators of Blue Ocean Strategy product and process performance that are important to and directly serve your customers? How do these results compare with the performance of your competitors and other organizations with similar offerings?
<--- Score

29. How familiar are you with the product development process?
<--- Score

30. How has the Blue Ocean Strategy data been gathered?
<--- Score

31. What tools were used to generate the list of possible causes?
<--- Score

32. What did the team gain from developing a sub-process map?
<--- Score

33. What kind of crime could a potential new hire have committed that would not only not disqualify him/her from being hired by your organization, but would actually indicate that he/she might be a particularly good fit?
<--- Score

34. What successful thing are you doing today that may be blinding you to new growth opportunities?
<--- Score

35. Is the performance gap determined?
<--- Score

36. How is Blue Ocean Strategy data gathered?
<--- Score

37. What methods do you use to gather Blue Ocean Strategy data?
<--- Score

38. What are the revised rough estimates of the financial savings/opportunity for Blue Ocean Strategy improvements?
<--- Score

39. Have the problem and goal statements been

updated to reflect the additional knowledge gained from the analyze phase?
<--- Score

40. Is data and process analysis, root cause analysis and quantifying the gap/opportunity in place?
<--- Score

41. How do you promote understanding that opportunity for improvement is not criticism of the status quo, or the people who created the status quo?
<--- Score

42. Were there any improvement opportunities identified from the process analysis?
<--- Score

43. How do you assure that your vendors are adequately qualified?
<--- Score

44. Was a cause-and-effect diagram used to explore the different types of causes (or sources of variation)?
<--- Score

45. How do you define collaboration and team output?
<--- Score

46. How often will data be collected for measures?
<--- Score

47. How difficult is it to qualify what Blue Ocean Strategy ROI is?
<--- Score

48. What quality tools were used to get through the analyze phase?
<--- Score

49. What do you need to qualify?
<--- Score

50. What does the data say about the performance of the stakeholder process?
<--- Score

51. What changes need to be made based on the data?
<--- Score

52. Will your data be confidential?
<--- Score

53. What were the crucial 'moments of truth' on the process map?
<--- Score

54. What key processes give you competitive advantage?
<--- Score

55. What data is gathered?
<--- Score

56. Were any designed experiments used to generate additional insight into the data analysis?
<--- Score

57. What is the complexity of the output produced?
<--- Score

58. Do your employees have the opportunity to do what they do best everyday?
<--- Score

59. What resources go in to get the desired output?
<--- Score

60. Are all team members qualified for all tasks?
<--- Score

61. Have you defined which data is gathered how?
<--- Score

62. Did any value-added analysis or 'lean thinking' take place to identify some of the gaps shown on the 'as is' process map?
<--- Score

63. What business opportunity do you choose?
<--- Score

64. How do you identify specific Blue Ocean Strategy investment opportunities and emerging trends?
<--- Score

65. Do your leaders quickly bounce back from setbacks?
<--- Score

66. What Blue Ocean Strategy metrics are outputs of the process?
<--- Score

67. How do you improve the utilization of a process?
<--- Score

68. Record-keeping requirements flow from the records needed as inputs, outputs, controls and for transformation of a Blue Ocean Strategy process. Are the records needed as inputs to the Blue Ocean Strategy process available?
<--- Score

69. How is the data gathered?
<--- Score

70. What qualifications are needed?
<--- Score

71. Is the gap/opportunity displayed and communicated in financial terms?
<--- Score

72. Where is the data coming from to measure compliance?
<--- Score

73. Where can you get qualified talent today?
<--- Score

74. Did any additional data need to be collected?
<--- Score

75. What is your organizations process which leads to recognition of value generation?
<--- Score

76. Is pre-qualification of suppliers carried out?
<--- Score

77. Are Blue Ocean Strategy changes recognized early

enough to be approved through the regular process?
<--- Score

78. Is the Blue Ocean Strategy process severely broken such that a re-design is necessary?
<--- Score

79. What tools were used to narrow the list of possible causes?
<--- Score

80. What are your key performance measures or indicators and in-process measures for the control and improvement of your Blue Ocean Strategy processes?
<--- Score

81. A compounding model resolution with available relevant data can often provide insight towards a solution methodology; which Blue Ocean Strategy models, tools and techniques are necessary?
<--- Score

82. What are your outputs?
<--- Score

83. What conclusions were drawn from the team's data collection and analysis? How did the team reach these conclusions?
<--- Score

84. What are the necessary qualifications?
<--- Score

85. Has an output goal been set?
<--- Score

86. What are the opportunities and threats on the distribution side?

<--- Score

87. Have any additional benefits been identified that will result from closing all or most of the gaps?

<--- Score

88. How good are your business processes?

<--- Score

89. What training and qualifications will you need?

<--- Score

90. What will drive Blue Ocean Strategy change?

<--- Score

91. How do you use Blue Ocean Strategy data and information to support organizational decision making and innovation?

<--- Score

Add up total points for this section:
_____ = Total points for this section

Divided by: _____ (number of statements answered) = _____
Average score for this section

Transfer your score to the Blue Ocean Strategy Index at the beginning of the Self-Assessment.

CRITERION #5: IMPROVE:

INTENT: Develop a practical solution. Innovate, establish and test the solution and to measure the results.

In my belief, the answer to this question is clearly defined:

5 Strongly Agree

4 Agree

3 Neutral

2 Disagree

1 Strongly Disagree

1. How do you define the solutions' scope?
<--- Score

2. In the past few months, what is the smallest change you have made that has had the biggest positive result? What was it about that small change that produced the large return?
<--- Score

3. Explorations of the frontiers of Blue Ocean Strategy will help you build influence, improve Blue Ocean Strategy, optimize decision making, and sustain change, what is your approach?
<--- Score

4. What tools were used to tap into the creativity and encourage 'outside the box' thinking?
<--- Score

5. Risk factors: what are the characteristics of Blue Ocean Strategy that make it risky?
<--- Score

6. For decision problems, how do you develop a decision statement?
<--- Score

7. Blue Ocean Strategy risk decisions: whose call Is It?
<--- Score

8. Is there a high likelihood that any recommendations will achieve their intended results?
<--- Score

9. What communications are necessary to support the implementation of the solution?
<--- Score

10. How do the Blue Ocean Strategy results compare with the performance of your competitors and other organizations with similar offerings?
<--- Score

11. Were any criteria developed to assist the team in testing and evaluating potential solutions?

<--- Score

12. What are your current levels and trends in key measures or indicators of workforce and leader development?
<--- Score

13. Who will be responsible for making the decisions to include or exclude requested changes once Blue Ocean Strategy is underway?
<--- Score

14. How will you know that a change is an improvement?
<--- Score

15. How will the team or the process owner(s) monitor the implementation plan to see that it is working as intended?
<--- Score

16. How do you develop new relationships?
<--- Score

17. Is the measure of success for Blue Ocean Strategy understandable to a variety of people?
<--- Score

18. What is the team's contingency plan for potential problems occurring in implementation?
<--- Score

19. How do you go about comparing Blue Ocean Strategy approaches/solutions?
<--- Score

20. What to do with the results or outcomes of measurements?
<--- Score

21. Are the best solutions selected?
<--- Score

22. Was a pilot designed for the proposed solution(s)?
<--- Score

23. Are improved process ('should be') maps modified based on pilot data and analysis?
<--- Score

24. What tools were most useful during the improve phase?
<--- Score

25. Who are the people involved in developing and implementing Blue Ocean Strategy?
<--- Score

26. Is the optimal solution selected based on testing and analysis?
<--- Score

27. Is there a cost/benefit analysis of optimal solution(s)?
<--- Score

28. How did the team generate the list of possible solutions?
<--- Score

29. Have you identified breakpoints and/or risk tolerances that will trigger broad consideration of

a potential need for intervention or modification of strategy?
<--- Score

30. What are past bad strategic business decisions?
<--- Score

31. Are new and improved process ('should be') maps developed?
<--- Score

32. What does the 'should be' process map/design look like?
<--- Score

33. What lessons, if any, from a pilot were incorporated into the design of the full-scale solution?
<--- Score

34. Who controls the risk?
<--- Score

35. What went well, what should change, what can improve?
<--- Score

36. What tools were used to evaluate the potential solutions?
<--- Score

37. What error proofing will be done to address some of the discrepancies observed in the 'as is' process?
<--- Score

38. Are there any constraints (technical, political, cultural, or otherwise) that would inhibit certain

solutions?
<--- Score

39. How do you link measurement and risk?
<--- Score

40. What is Blue Ocean Strategy's impact on utilizing the best solution(s)?
<--- Score

41. Is your strategy screen consistently used in all decision making?
<--- Score

42. What are the implications of the one critical Blue Ocean Strategy decision 10 minutes, 10 months, and 10 years from now?
<--- Score

43. Is a solution implementation plan established, including schedule/work breakdown structure, resources, risk management plan, cost/budget, and control plan?
<--- Score

44. How do your managers develop a sustainable strategy in fast-changing environments?
<--- Score

45. Who makes decisions about the issue?
<--- Score

46. Is a contingency plan established?
<--- Score

47. How do you decide how much to remunerate an

employee?
<--- Score

48. Are possible solutions generated and tested?
<--- Score

49. How will the group know that the solution worked?
<--- Score

50. Who do you report Blue Ocean Strategy results to?
<--- Score

51. In developing and managing products how do you decide what customers want?
<--- Score

52. Is this a strategic decision?
<--- Score

53. How will you measure the results?
<--- Score

54. Is the solution technically practical?
<--- Score

55. Is pilot data collected and analyzed?
<--- Score

56. What actually has to improve and by how much?
<--- Score

57. Describe the design of the pilot and what tests were conducted, if any?
<--- Score

58. Is there a small-scale pilot for proposed improvement(s)? What conclusions were drawn from the outcomes of a pilot?
<--- Score

59. Who will be using the results of the measurement activities?
<--- Score

60. What do you want to improve?
<--- Score

61. What can you do to improve?
<--- Score

62. How will you know when its improved?
<--- Score

63. Does a good decision guarantee a good outcome?
<--- Score

64. Are risk triggers captured?
<--- Score

65. Are the decisions based on appropriate facts?
<--- Score

66. Who controls key decisions that will be made?
<--- Score

67. How do you counsel your organization to improve its creative executions?
<--- Score

68. Risk events: what are the things that could go wrong?

<--- Score

69. Who will be responsible for documenting the Blue Ocean Strategy requirements in detail?
<--- Score

70. What were the underlying assumptions on the cost-benefit analysis?
<--- Score

71. How will you know that you have improved?
<--- Score

72. Is the implementation plan designed?
<--- Score

73. How does the team improve its work?
<--- Score

74. How can you reduce your risk?
<--- Score

75. Do you combine technical expertise with business knowledge and Blue Ocean Strategy Key topics include lifecycles, development approaches, requirements and how to make a business case?
<--- Score

76. What is the implementation plan?
<--- Score

77. How do you manage and improve your Blue Ocean Strategy work systems to deliver customer value and achieve organizational success and sustainability?
<--- Score

78. What improvements have been achieved?
<--- Score

79. How does the solution remove the key sources of issues discovered in the analyze phase?
<--- Score

80. How risky is your organization?
<--- Score

81. What resources are required for the improvement efforts?
<--- Score

82. What attendant changes will need to be made to ensure that the solution is successful?
<--- Score

83. How do you improve your likelihood of success ?
<--- Score

Add up total points for this section:
_____ = Total points for this section

Divided by: _____ (number of statements answered) = _____
Average score for this section

Transfer your score to the Blue Ocean Strategy Index at the beginning of the Self-Assessment.

CRITERION #6: CONTROL:

INTENT: Implement the practical solution. Maintain the performance and correct possible complications.

In my belief, the answer to this question is clearly defined:

5 Strongly Agree

4 Agree

3 Neutral

2 Disagree

1 Strongly Disagree

1. What quality tools were useful in the control phase?
<--- Score

2. How can you best use all of your knowledge repositories to enhance learning and sharing?
<--- Score

3. Does a troubleshooting guide exist or is it needed?
<--- Score

4. Are operating procedures consistent?
<--- Score

5. What are the critical parameters to watch?
<--- Score

6. In the case of a Blue Ocean Strategy project, the criteria for the audit derive from implementation objectives. an audit of a Blue Ocean Strategy project involves assessing whether the recommendations outlined for implementation have been met. Can you track that any Blue Ocean Strategy project is implemented as planned, and is it working?
<--- Score

7. How do you establish and deploy modified action plans if circumstances require a shift in plans and rapid execution of new plans?
<--- Score

8. What is your theory of human motivation, and how does your compensation plan fit with that view?
<--- Score

9. Is a response plan in place for when the input, process, or output measures indicate an 'out-of-control' condition?
<--- Score

10. Are there documented procedures?
<--- Score

11. What is the recommended frequency of auditing?
<--- Score

12. What other areas of the group might benefit from the Blue Ocean Strategy team's improvements, knowledge, and learning?
<--- Score

13. When it is your responsibility to organize and plan a project, what steps do you take?
<--- Score

14. Are documented procedures clear and easy to follow for the operators?
<--- Score

15. How do controls support value?
<--- Score

16. How will the process owner verify improvement in present and future sigma levels, process capabilities?
<--- Score

17. How will report readings be checked to effectively monitor performance?
<--- Score

18. Is a response plan established and deployed?
<--- Score

19. How do you plan for the cost of succession?
<--- Score

20. Which factors should be reduced well below the industrys standard?
<--- Score

21. How is change control managed?
<--- Score

22. Does the response plan contain a definite closed loop continual improvement scheme (e.g., plan-do-check-act)?
<--- Score

23. Is there documentation that will support the successful operation of the improvement?
<--- Score

24. What is the control/monitoring plan?
<--- Score

25. What do you measure to verify effectiveness gains?
<--- Score

26. How will new or emerging customer needs/requirements be checked/communicated to orient the process toward meeting the new specifications and continually reducing variation?
<--- Score

27. Who is the Blue Ocean Strategy process owner?
<--- Score

28. Are you measuring, monitoring and predicting Blue Ocean Strategy activities to optimize operations and profitability, and enhancing outcomes?
<--- Score

29. What other systems, operations, processes, and infrastructures (hiring practices, staffing, training, incentives/rewards, metrics/dashboards/scorecards, etc.) need updates, additions, changes, or deletions in order to facilitate knowledge transfer and

improvements?
<--- Score

30. How will input, process, and output variables be checked to detect for sub-optimal conditions?
<--- Score

31. Will existing staff require re-training, for example, to learn new business processes?
<--- Score

32. Who will be in control?
<--- Score

33. How might the group capture best practices and lessons learned so as to leverage improvements?
<--- Score

34. How will you measure your QA plan's effectiveness?
<--- Score

35. What key inputs and outputs are being measured on an ongoing basis?
<--- Score

36. How do you encourage people to take control and responsibility?
<--- Score

37. Have new or revised work instructions resulted?
<--- Score

38. Which are the controlling forces for profitability?
<--- Score

39. Which factors should be raised above the industrys standard?

<--- Score

40. Is new knowledge gained imbedded in the response plan?

<--- Score

41. What should you measure to verify efficiency gains?

<--- Score

42. Do you monitor the Blue Ocean Strategy decisions made and fine tune them as they evolve?

<--- Score

43. What metrics help you monitor performance after release?

<--- Score

44. What should the next improvement project be that is related to Blue Ocean Strategy?

<--- Score

45. Is there a recommended audit plan for routine surveillance inspections of Blue Ocean Strategy's gains?

<--- Score

46. What can you control?

<--- Score

47. How will Blue Ocean Strategy decisions be made and monitored?

<--- Score

48. Will any special training be provided for results interpretation?
<--- Score

49. How will the process owner and team be able to hold the gains?
<--- Score

50. Which standards should be raised well above the industrys standard?
<--- Score

51. Is there a Blue Ocean Strategy Communication plan covering who needs to get what information when?
<--- Score

52. Who controls critical resources?
<--- Score

53. Are controls in place and consistently applied?
<--- Score

54. Who controls the budget for the product you are selling?
<--- Score

55. Are pertinent alerts monitored, analyzed and distributed to appropriate personnel?
<--- Score

56. Is reporting being used or needed?
<--- Score

57. What do you plan to achieve?

<--- Score

58. Will the team be available to assist members in planning investigations?
<--- Score

59. Is there a documented and implemented monitoring plan?
<--- Score

60. Are suggested corrective/restorative actions indicated on the response plan for known causes to problems that might surface?
<--- Score

61. Does job training on the documented procedures need to be part of the process team's education and training?
<--- Score

62. Is there a transfer of ownership and knowledge to process owner and process team tasked with the responsibilities.
<--- Score

63. Is knowledge gained on process shared and institutionalized?
<--- Score

64. Does the Blue Ocean Strategy performance meet the customer's requirements?
<--- Score

65. How will the day-to-day responsibilities for monitoring and continual improvement be transferred from the improvement team to the

process owner?
<--- Score

66. Where do ideas that reach policy makers and planners as proposals for Blue Ocean Strategy strengthening and reform actually originate?
<--- Score

67. How is the control of critical digital assets being addressed with regard to safety and security?
<--- Score

68. Are new process steps, standards, and documentation ingrained into normal operations?
<--- Score

69. What do you stand for--and what are you against?
<--- Score

70. Do the Blue Ocean Strategy decisions you make today help people and the planet tomorrow?
<--- Score

71. Is there a control plan in place for sustaining improvements (short and long-term)?
<--- Score

72. How do you plan on providing proper recognition and disclosure of supporting companies?
<--- Score

73. Does Blue Ocean Strategy appropriately measure and monitor risk?
<--- Score

74. Is there an action plan in case of emergencies?
<--- Score

75. Has the improved process and its steps been standardized?
<--- Score

76. Is there a standardized process?
<--- Score

77. Which factors should be reduced below the industrys standard?
<--- Score

78. How do you select, collect, align, and integrate Blue Ocean Strategy data and information for tracking daily operations and overall organizational performance, including progress relative to strategic objectives and action plans?
<--- Score

Add up total points for this section:
_ _ _ _ _ = Total points for this section

Divided by: _ _ _ _ _ _ (number of statements answered) = _ _ _ _ _ _
Average score for this section

Transfer your score to the Blue Ocean Strategy Index at the beginning of the Self-Assessment.

CRITERION #7: SUSTAIN:

INTENT: Retain the benefits.

In my belief, the answer to this question is clearly defined:

5 Strongly Agree

4 Agree

3 Neutral

2 Disagree

1 Strongly Disagree

1. What financial tools can you use to realize the changes?
<--- Score

2. What are the red ocean traps?
<--- Score

3. How blue is your strategy?
<--- Score

4. What must you excel at?

<--- Score

5. Who are the key stakeholders?
<--- Score

6. Are product life cycles really getting shorter?
<--- Score

7. If you find that you havent accomplished one of the goals for one of the steps of the Blue Ocean Strategy strategy, what will you do to fix it?
<--- Score

8. Is Blue Ocean Strategy dependent on the successful delivery of a current project?
<--- Score

9. Can you account for quantitative value proposition?
<--- Score

10. What factors must be raised or created?
<--- Score

11. When does a differentiation strategy work best?
<--- Score

12. How do you maximize the size of the blue ocean you are creating?
<--- Score

13. What projects are going on in the organization today, and what resources are those projects using from the resource pools?
<--- Score

14. Which factors that the industry has never offered should be created?

<--- Score

15. What are your staff and financial resources?

<--- Score

16. What factors should be created that are new to the industry?

<--- Score

17. What is the overall business strategy?

<--- Score

18. What makes a leader?

<--- Score

19. How do you track customer value, profitability or financial return, organizational success, and sustainability?

<--- Score

20. How do you motivate people?

<--- Score

21. What are the pros and cons of remaining independent?

<--- Score

22. How would a major influx of foreign business affect things?

<--- Score

23. Who are your customers?

<--- Score

24. Does your strategy take into account competitor action and reaction?

<--- Score

25. What are your short-term and long-term campaign objectives?

<--- Score

26. What Blue Ocean Strategy modifications can you make work for you?

<--- Score

27. What are the success criteria that will indicate that Blue Ocean Strategy objectives have been met and the benefits delivered?

<--- Score

28. How does your strategy relate to sustainable competitive advantage?

<--- Score

29. How will you know your blue ocean is turning red?

<--- Score

30. How will your organizations vision of being the best organization in your organization prevail?

<--- Score

31. How do you share the workload?

<--- Score

32. When and how should your organization diversify?

<--- Score

33. Is there any existing Blue Ocean Strategy governance structure?
<--- Score

34. What obstacles might your organization face in pursuing a strategy that involves an online, virtual world?
<--- Score

35. What are the strategic functions of innovation?
<--- Score

36. What is the appropriate degree of conservatism?
<--- Score

37. What influences the success of your organization?
<--- Score

38. What is the consumer testing indicating?
<--- Score

39. How does your organization adapt to the change?
<--- Score

40. Is a Blue Ocean Strategy team work effort in place?
<--- Score

41. How to best leverage private or state investment?
<--- Score

42. Which uncustomers do not buy from you and

should?
<--- Score

43. What level of coordination exists, and why not more?
<--- Score

44. Who will determine interim and final deadlines?
<--- Score

45. How do you ensure that implementations of Blue Ocean Strategy products are done in a way that ensures safety?
<--- Score

46. What knowledge, skills and characteristics mark a good Blue Ocean Strategy project manager?
<--- Score

47. Is it an attractive industry?
<--- Score

48. Why do you have to choose?
<--- Score

49. How will you know that the Blue Ocean Strategy project has been successful?
<--- Score

50. For what value are your customers really willing to pay ?
<--- Score

51. How do senior leaders deploy your organizations vision and values through your leadership system, to the workforce, to key suppliers and partners, and to

customers and other stakeholders, as appropriate?
<--- Score

52. What stupid rule would you most like to kill?
<--- Score

53. How do you test the idea in the beginning?
<--- Score

54. What is your strategy screen?
<--- Score

55. How well is your organizations current Strategy working ?
<--- Score

56. What did you miss in the interview for the worst hire you ever made?
<--- Score

57. How do you foster the skills, knowledge, talents, attributes, and characteristics you want to have?
<--- Score

58. What emotion do you want to invoke?
<--- Score

59. If you got fired and a new hire took your place, what would she do different?
<--- Score

60. How would you determine if a given product is successful?
<--- Score

61. Why use innovation to change the game of

business?

<--- Score

62. Who are trusted leaders for your audience?

<--- Score

63. Where can you break convention?

<--- Score

64. What do you take for granted that should be eliminated?

<--- Score

65. What does it take to be a successful ceo and leader?

<--- Score

66. How are you doing compared to your industry?

<--- Score

67. What does consumer behavior in later life look like?

<--- Score

68. How can your business be in a league of its own?

<--- Score

69. What counts that you are not counting?

<--- Score

70. Does your industry compete on functionality or emotional appeal?

<--- Score

71. Who has this power?

<--- Score

72. What was the vision of the founder?
<--- Score

73. Do incentives create innovation?
<--- Score

74. Why search for a new paradigm?
<--- Score

75. What is it like in a Red Ocean?
<--- Score

76. Which of your product or service varieties are the most distinctive?
<--- Score

77. Does your strategy exploit your key resources?
<--- Score

78. What are the adoption hurdles in actualizing your business idea?
<--- Score

79. Is Blue Ocean Strategy realistic, or are you setting yourself up for failure?
<--- Score

80. What is your organizations threat management?
<--- Score

81. What industry are you in?
<--- Score

82. Are there any established brand identities in your industry?

<--- Score

83. What is the Value Stream Mapping?

<--- Score

84. How does your business make this market better?

<--- Score

85. Who do we want your customers to become?

<--- Score

86. What is the kind of project structure that would be appropriate for your Blue Ocean Strategy project, should it be formal and complex, or can it be less formal and relatively simple?

<--- Score

87. What unique value proposition (UVP) do you offer?

<--- Score

88. How do you create value?

<--- Score

89. Do you see it?

<--- Score

90. How do you attract non-customers?

<--- Score

91. Does your strategy fit with what is going on in the environment?

<--- Score

92. Is the blue ocean strategy valid and reliable?
<--- Score

93. What projects/programs do you retain or implement?
<--- Score

94. How could the incentives for innovation arise?
<--- Score

95. What are the potential basics of Blue Ocean Strategy fraud?
<--- Score

96. Are you / should you be revolutionary or evolutionary?
<--- Score

97. If there were zero limitations, what would you do differently?
<--- Score

98. How do you ensure adherence to quality/service protocols?
<--- Score

99. How will you insure seamless interoperability of Blue Ocean Strategy moving forward?
<--- Score

100. How do you make your organization stand out?
<--- Score

101. What value is each Customer Segment truly willing to pay ?

<--- Score

102. What are the strategic groups in your industry?

<--- Score

103. What are the technology enablers of the strategy?

<--- Score

104. How do you proactively clarify deliverables and Blue Ocean Strategy quality expectations?

<--- Score

105. How should your organization be positioned?

<--- Score

106. What is an unauthorized commitment?

<--- Score

107. Does it make sense for the customer ?

<--- Score

108. What are the key factors for competitive success?

<--- Score

109. What approaches to growth preserve and reinforce strategy?

<--- Score

110. What is the purpose of Blue Ocean Strategy in relation to the mission?

<--- Score

111. Why does it matter?

<--- Score

112. How can you change the environment?
<--- Score

113. How can it be summarized?
<--- Score

114. What alternatives do you consider?
<--- Score

115. Who are the best positioned players?
<--- Score

116. Why not do Blue Ocean Strategy?
<--- Score

117. What is the chain of buyers in your industry?
<--- Score

118. Is the concept of the blue ocean strategy unique?
<--- Score

119. What potential megatrends could make your business model obsolete?
<--- Score

120. Is there exceptional unique quality in the business idea?
<--- Score

121. What are you supposed to do?
<--- Score

122. Can you do this outside of your country?

<--- Score

123. How do you make money?
<--- Score

124. What do you want to achieve over the long term?
<--- Score

125. What is the overall talent health of your organization as a whole at senior levels, and for each organization reporting to a member of the Senior Leadership Team?
<--- Score

126. What is your brands positioning?
<--- Score

127. How does your experience influence your thinking?
<--- Score

128. What is your Blue Ocean Strategy strategy?
<--- Score

129. What core values do you share with the people you want to influence?
<--- Score

130. How will new trends play out?
<--- Score

131. Do you choose Blue ocean or fast-second innovation?
<--- Score

132. What tangible outcomes would you like to achieve through a communications effort?
<--- Score

133. How are management fashions organizationalized?
<--- Score

134. How long does it take to get the product delivered?
<--- Score

135. What does the customer really want?
<--- Score

136. How do you engage the workforce, in addition to satisfying them?
<--- Score

137. What are the goals of the new strategy?
<--- Score

138. Whom among your colleagues do you trust, and for what?
<--- Score

139. Where do clients have trouble finding products?
<--- Score

140. How do the different market players view the evolving ecosystem?
<--- Score

141. Who are the Non-Consumers of the targeted industry?

<--- Score

142. What vulnerability exists to changes in the industry?
<--- Score

143. Which elements should be increased to be above the industry norms?
<--- Score

144. What is the positioning challenge?
<--- Score

145. Why is it a competitive advantage?
<--- Score

146. Which factors should be created that the industry has never offered?
<--- Score

147. When and how will incentives for innovation appear?
<--- Score

148. Does your business idea offer exceptional utility to the buyer?
<--- Score

149. What challenges do you face in your community?
<--- Score

150. Is the Blue Ocean Strategy organization completing tasks effectively and efficiently?
<--- Score

151. Does your group have allies (or opponents)?
<--- Score

152. Does your strategy help you say no?
<--- Score

153. When is it time to man the life boats?
<--- Score

154. Which of your customers are the most satisfied?
<--- Score

155. Who are the competitors, and what are their strengths and weaknesses?
<--- Score

156. Are the elements of your strategy internally consistent?
<--- Score

157. Why the dramatic imbalance in favor of red oceans?
<--- Score

158. How is your strategy consistent with your Value Proposition ?
<--- Score

159. How do your consumers screen advertisements?
<--- Score

160. Is consumer demand kinked?
<--- Score

161. Who is using your products in ways you never expected?

<--- Score

162. How do you get a grip on competing in a Fragmented Industry ?

<--- Score

163. Will customers accept the new product, service or marketing approach?

<--- Score

164. How are external services linked to internal?

<--- Score

165. Where are the limits of the differentiation strategy ?

<--- Score

166. How do you overcome the obstacles?

<--- Score

167. Do you have the money to spend on the necessary changes?

<--- Score

168. How do the incentives for innovation arise?

<--- Score

169. Who influences a sale and who recommends it?

<--- Score

170. What trouble can you get into?

<--- Score

171. What are current Blue Ocean Strategy paradigms?
<--- Score

172. What are you challenging?
<--- Score

173. Who are four people whose careers you have enhanced?
<--- Score

174. Is the right innovation strategy to position your organization as a fast follower?
<--- Score

175. Is your strategy ambitious, or does it allow you to coast?
<--- Score

176. How can you become the company that would put you out of business?
<--- Score

177. Who are your key suppliers?
<--- Score

178. What are strategies for increasing support and reducing opposition?
<--- Score

179. What trophy do you want on your mantle?
<--- Score

180. How do you acquire, keep and grow customers?
<--- Score

181. Which forces are underpinning (or constraining) todays profitability?

<--- Score

182. Why do so many companies fail to have a strategy?

<--- Score

183. What are the key enablers to make this Blue Ocean Strategy move?

<--- Score

184. What does that mean for future business models?

<--- Score

185. What is the unique value that you can build on?

<--- Score

186. What ethics variable is most important in doing business?

<--- Score

187. How do you effectively cater to the older consumer?

<--- Score

188. What makes blue ocean strategy imperative for global companies today?

<--- Score

189. Do you have to take part?

<--- Score

190. How effective are features and functions?

<--- Score

191. What are your organizations mission, objectives, and distinctive competency?
<--- Score

192. Do you think you know, or do you know you know ?
<--- Score

193. How difficult is it to unpack and install the new product?
<--- Score

194. What are the trends in distribution in each of your market segments?
<--- Score

195. Where or from whom does your audience get its information?
<--- Score

196. How do customers see your organization?
<--- Score

197. Are you following or running away from the market leader?
<--- Score

198. How long to get the product delivered?
<--- Score

199. Can you clearly and concisely state what your strategy is?
<--- Score

200. What happens if you do not have enough funding?
<--- Score

201. What are the industrys dominant economic traits?
<--- Score

202. If you were responsible for initiating and implementing major changes in your organization, what steps might you take to ensure acceptance of those changes?
<--- Score

203. In ways do you challenge managements ideas and assumptions?
<--- Score

204. What does your customer segment expect?
<--- Score

205. Where does the profit come from?
<--- Score

206. Is one or another of your objectives time-dependent?
<--- Score

207. If you had to rebuild your organization without any traditional competitive advantages (i.e., no killer technology, promising research, innovative product/service delivery model, etc.), how would your people have to approach their work and collaborate together in order to create the necessary conditions for success?
<--- Score

208. Why should you find your blue ocean?
<--- Score

209. Think of your Blue Ocean Strategy project, what are the main functions?
<--- Score

210. How will you know if you are on course?
<--- Score

211. Whose voice (department, ethnic group, women, older workers, etc) might you have missed hearing from in your company, and how might you amplify this voice to create positive momentum for your business?
<--- Score

212. Political -is anyone trying to undermine this project?
<--- Score

213. What is the positioning chosen by your organization in each of its segment ?
<--- Score

214. Why is it important to have senior management support for a Blue Ocean Strategy project?
<--- Score

215. What is the funding source for this project?
<--- Score

216. What are the barriers that may hinder your organizations innovation?
<--- Score

217. For some of your projects, are there companies copying you?

<--- Score

218. How well is your organizations present strategy working?

<--- Score

219. What will reinforce the communitys view of you as a resource of choice?

<--- Score

220. What is your future competition strategy?

<--- Score

221. Why does that make you better?

<--- Score

222. How dynamic can organizational capabilities be?

<--- Score

223. Can support from partners be adjusted?

<--- Score

224. How do you make this work within the system?

<--- Score

225. Are the assumptions used accurate?

<--- Score

226. When is it the right time to find your blue ocean strategy?

<--- Score

227. Why will customers want to buy your organizations products/services?
<--- Score

228. Does your strategy differ per customer segment ?
<--- Score

229. How is your pricing strategy conducted?
<--- Score

230. What are other industries doing that you can adopt or enhance?
<--- Score

231. How do you lead with Blue Ocean Strategy in mind?
<--- Score

232. How easy is it to dispose of the product?
<--- Score

233. Is it consistent with your mission?
<--- Score

234. What colour is your strategy?
<--- Score

235. How will you educate customers to become more price-conscious?
<--- Score

236. Is your organization ready for blue ocean strategies?
<--- Score

237. How effective are the products features and functions?

<--- Score

238. How you can differentiate the Value Proposition ?

<--- Score

239. What should management do?

<--- Score

240. How familiar are you with product's lifecycle management?

<--- Score

241. What is the one, specific thing that you want your target audience to do?

<--- Score

242. So you kind of expand the game for your business?

<--- Score

243. What do you find waiting in a Red Ocean marketplace?

<--- Score

244. How do you reach the audiences you targeted?

<--- Score

245. How will you motivate the stakeholders with the least vested interest?

<--- Score

246. What is different about your blue ocean?
<--- Score

247. What is your BATNA (best alternative to a negotiated agreement)?
<--- Score

248. Which elements should be reduced to be below the industry norms?
<--- Score

249. Are you priced right for your client and your business?
<--- Score

250. Who has the power, influence, or authority to give you what you want?
<--- Score

251. When is it time to execute a Blue Ocean Strategy?
<--- Score

252. Who is the main stakeholder, with ultimate responsibility for driving Blue Ocean Strategy forward?
<--- Score

253. If no one would ever find out about your accomplishments, how would you lead differently?
<--- Score

254. How viable is this approach?
<--- Score

255. How do you get customers?

<--- Score

256. What is red, what is blue?
<--- Score

257. How do you employ strategic alliances or collaborative partnerships ?
<--- Score

258. How sustainable is a Blue Ocean Strategy?
<--- Score

259. Do you have a new potential partnership in the distribution?
<--- Score

260. What are the reasons for cooperation in innovation?
<--- Score

261. What are the short and long-term Blue Ocean Strategy goals?
<--- Score

262. How do you accomplish your long range Blue Ocean Strategy goals?
<--- Score

263. What market positions do rivals occupy?
<--- Score

264. What are the market segments chosen by your organization ?
<--- Score

**265. What would it take to ensure that each

customer is highly satisfied?
<--- Score

266. When you have excess liquidity, what do you invest in?
<--- Score

267. What business benefits will Blue Ocean Strategy goals deliver if achieved?
<--- Score

268. Will it not put you in competition with your essential partners?
<--- Score

269. Do you value your employees?
<--- Score

270. Can the market be segmented?
<--- Score

271. What is the sales cycle of the considered channels?
<--- Score

272. What review/metrics do you use?
<--- Score

273. Is this an ethical strategy?
<--- Score

274. What do your employees/customers/partners believe?
<--- Score

275. Why is this important?

<--- Score

276. What are your most important goals for the strategic Blue Ocean Strategy objectives?

<--- Score

277. What do you have to offer?

<--- Score

278. Do you review your strategy regularly?

<--- Score

279. What competing factors are considered valid in the strategy canvas?

<--- Score

280. What are you trying to prove to yourself, and how might it be hijacking your life and business success?

<--- Score

281. How are you integrating your products with customer routines?

<--- Score

282. How do you question your organizations current strategy or position?

<--- Score

283. What is the pricing positioning of your organization ?

<--- Score

284. What happens when a new employee joins the organization?

<--- Score

285. Who, on the executive team or the board, has spoken to a customer recently?
<--- Score

286. Do you merge with or acquire other companies ?
<--- Score

287. How do you provide a safe environment -physically and emotionally?
<--- Score

288. What are the adoption hurdles in actualising the business idea?
<--- Score

289. What can you do to protect your community?
<--- Score

290. How do you maintain Blue Ocean Strategy's Integrity?
<--- Score

291. What is the value proposition that distinguishes you?
<--- Score

292. Who is going to gauge the business health?
<--- Score

293. Are the assumptions believable and achievable?
<--- Score

294. What are the business goals Blue Ocean Strategy is aiming to achieve?
<--- Score

295. Which organization would be appropriate to benchmark?

<--- Score

296. In a project to restructure Blue Ocean Strategy outcomes, which stakeholders would you involve?

<--- Score

297. Sustainability strategies: when does it pay to be green?

<--- Score

298. Who are your partners?

<--- Score

299. Which Blue Ocean Strategy goals are the most important?

<--- Score

300. Can the schedule be done in the given time?

<--- Score

301. What is the source of the strategies for Blue Ocean Strategy strengthening and reform?

<--- Score

302. Instead of going to current contacts for new ideas, what if you reconnected with dormant contacts--the people you used to know? If you were going reactivate a dormant tie, who would it be?

<--- Score

303. How do you excel?

<--- Score

304. Is it good for your organizations', and your, reputation?
<--- Score

305. If you do not follow, then how to lead?
<--- Score

306. What is the probability that this product fails?
<--- Score

307. Who is it for?
<--- Score

308. Which factors should be created that the industry never offered?
<--- Score

309. What will be the consequences to the stakeholder (financial, reputation etc) if Blue Ocean Strategy does not go ahead or fails to deliver the objectives?
<--- Score

310. Is there a work around that you can use?
<--- Score

311. Is your group/topic/goal known about and being considered?
<--- Score

312. Is your group in agreement on its goals and objectives?
<--- Score

313. What goals did you miss?
<--- Score

314. What happens at your organization when people fail?

<--- Score

315. In your industry is the pioneer advantage marketing logic or marketing legend?

<--- Score

316. What can be created that the industry does not offer?

<--- Score

317. What may be the consequences for the performance of an organization if all stakeholders are not consulted regarding Blue Ocean Strategy?

<--- Score

318. Is your strategy driving your strategy? Or is the way in which you allocate resources driving your strategy?

<--- Score

319. What are the top 3 things at the forefront of your Blue Ocean Strategy agendas for the next 3 years?

<--- Score

320. Which of your product or service varieties are the most profitable?

<--- Score

321. Is there any reason to believe the opposite of my current belief?

<--- Score

322. What are the rules and assumptions your industry

operates under? What if the opposite were true?
<--- Score

323. How is implementation research currently incorporated into each of your goals?
<--- Score

324. What do you do that is hard to copy?
<--- Score

325. Should you be revising an old business model?
<--- Score

326. What are adoption hurdles in actualizing your business idea?
<--- Score

327. How do you want them to feel?
<--- Score

328. Who will be responsible for deciding whether Blue Ocean Strategy goes ahead or not after the initial investigations?
<--- Score

329. What market type are you dealing with?
<--- Score

330. How has your educational background and experience prepared you for the work you do?
<--- Score

331. How likely is it that a customer would recommend your company to a friend or colleague?
<--- Score

332. What are the greatest obstacles to adoption of your strategy over the next 5 years?
<--- Score

333. Which customers or markets will you target?
<--- Score

334. In retrospect, of the projects that you pulled the plug on, what percent do you wish had been allowed to keep going, and what percent do you wish had ended earlier?
<--- Score

335. What forces are driving change in the industry?
<--- Score

336. Why a blue ocean strategy?
<--- Score

337. How easy is it to maintain and upgrade the product?
<--- Score

338. How do you deal with Blue Ocean Strategy changes?
<--- Score

339. Which is an internal threat?
<--- Score

340. What would happen if you start from scratch?
<--- Score

341. What factors have contributed to the present

situation?
<--- Score

342. How do you calculate market share?
<--- Score

343. Who is responsible for errors?
<--- Score

344. Do you feel that more should be done in the Blue Ocean Strategy area?
<--- Score

345. What value will you deliver to the customer ?
<--- Score

346. Does this leverage your core competencies?
<--- Score

347. Which functions and people interact with the supplier and or customer?
<--- Score

348. Is your basic point _____ or _____?
<--- Score

349. How do you communicate and reach your Customer Segment?
<--- Score

350. How do senior leaders actions reflect a commitment to the organizations Blue Ocean Strategy values?
<--- Score

351. Where does your audience spend most of its

time?
<--- Score

352. Which customers, channels, or purchase occasions are the most profitable?
<--- Score

353. Do you have a flow diagram of what happens?
<--- Score

354. How do you win?
<--- Score

355. Who else should you help?
<--- Score

356. How will you ensure you get what you expected?
<--- Score

357. How do you market to the ultimate consumer?
<--- Score

358. What are the incentives that could encourage your organization to engage in innovation?
<--- Score

359. Has the customers preference changed?
<--- Score

360. How do you set Blue Ocean Strategy stretch targets and how do you get people to not only participate in setting these stretch targets but also that they strive to achieve these?
<--- Score

361. Through which channels do your customer segments want to be reached ?
<--- Score

362. What are the barriers to your audience fully supporting or participating in reaching your goal?
<--- Score

363. Would you rather sell to knowledgeable and informed customers or to uninformed customers?
<--- Score

364. Are you sure you have a Strategy?
<--- Score

365. What are the alternative industries to your industry?
<--- Score

366. Does it make sense to be more efficient to market?
<--- Score

367. What are specific Blue Ocean Strategy rules to follow?
<--- Score

368. How would your co-workers describe your communication style?
<--- Score

369. Marketing budgets are tighter, consumers are more skeptical, and social media has changed forever the way we talk about Blue Ocean Strategy. How do you gain traction?
<--- Score

370. Do you think recession could encourage you to do more innovation?

<--- Score

371. How do you know if you are successful?

<--- Score

372. Can you change and/or design culture?

<--- Score

373. If you build it, will it be financially feasible?

<--- Score

374. What new services of functionality will be implemented next with Blue Ocean Strategy ?

<--- Score

375. What are the signals for your organization to innovate?

<--- Score

376. When is it possible to integrate this strategy?

<--- Score

377. How do you keep records, of what?

<--- Score

378. Will the new business model disrupt competitors?

<--- Score

379. What is it like to work for you?

<--- Score

380. What is the minimum viable product that the

customer will be interested in?
<--- Score

381. What is the recommended frequency of auditing?
<--- Score

382. How attractive is the industry from a profit perspective?
<--- Score

383. Is your red ocean strategy working for you?
<--- Score

384. What is the differentiator in your business?
<--- Score

385. Is there exceptional buyer utility in your business idea?
<--- Score

386. To whom do you add value?
<--- Score

387. What was the business model, in the very beginning?
<--- Score

388. Ask yourself: how would you do this work if you only had one staff member to do it?
<--- Score

389. Where are you looking?
<--- Score

390. Does use of the product create waste items?
<--- Score

391. Is your business built to take you there?

<--- Score

392. What do you look for?

<--- Score

393. Is your Blue ocean strategy specific to radical innovation?

<--- Score

394. For which value are customers willing to pay?

<--- Score

395. Will there be any necessary staff changes (redundancies or new hires)?

<--- Score

396. Who will provide the final approval of Blue Ocean Strategy deliverables?

<--- Score

397. How will you collect feedback?

<--- Score

398. How fast can you deploy a new sales force?

<--- Score

399. How widespread is its use?

<--- Score

400. Who of your competitors is in a blue ocean that you are not seeing yet?

<--- Score

401. If you had to leave your organization for a year

and the only communication you could have with employees/colleagues was a single paragraph, what would you write?
<--- Score

402. Why do and why don't your customers like your organization?
<--- Score

403. Who is the ideal target consumer?
<--- Score

404. When you move your organization from a luxury market to a normal market, do you think you expand the boundary of market in which your organization is operating?
<--- Score

Add up total points for this section:
_____ = Total points for this section

Divided by: _____ (number of statements answered) = _____
Average score for this section

Transfer your score to the Blue Ocean Strategy Index at the beginning of the Self-Assessment.

Blue Ocean Strategy and Managing Projects, Criteria for Project Managers:

1.0 Initiating Process Group: Blue Ocean Strategy

1. Information sharing?

2. How should needs be met?

3. Are you just doing busywork to pass the time?

4. What do they need to know about the Blue Ocean Strategy project?

5. Do you know if the Blue Ocean Strategy project requires outside equipment or vendor resources?

6. How will it affect me?

7. How is each deliverable reviewed, verified, and validated?

8. Although the Blue Ocean Strategy project manager does not directly manage procurement and contracting activities, who does manage procurement and contracting activities in your organization then if not the PM?

9. Professionals want to know what is expected from them what are the deliverables?

10. Contingency planning. if a risk event occurs, what will you do?

11. Have the stakeholders identified all individual requirements pertaining to business process?

12. What were things that you need to improve?

13. What is the NEXT thing to do?

14. How well did the chosen processes produce the expected results?

15. How well did you do?

16. What are the required resources?

17. Do you understand the quality and control criteria that must be achieved for successful Blue Ocean Strategy project completion?

18. What will you do?

19. Will the Blue Ocean Strategy project meet the client requirements, and will it achieve the business success criteria that justified doing the Blue Ocean Strategy project in the first place?

20. If action is called for, what form should it take?

1.1 Project Charter: Blue Ocean Strategy

21. Review the general mission What system will be affected by the improvement efforts?

22. Are there special technology requirements?

23. Major high-level milestone targets: what events measure progress?

24. Did your Blue Ocean Strategy project ask for this?

25. What date will the task finish?

26. Market – identify products market, including whether it is outside of the objective: what is the purpose of the program or Blue Ocean Strategy project?

27. What are the assigned resources?

28. Will this replace an existing product?

29. What material?

30. Whose input and support will this Blue Ocean Strategy project require?

31. What are you striving to accomplish (measurable goal(s))?

32. Blue Ocean Strategy project objective statement:

what must the Blue Ocean Strategy project do?

33. What ideas do you have for initial tests of change (PDSA cycles)?

34. Who is the Blue Ocean Strategy project Manager?

35. What metrics could you look at?

36. What does it need to do?

37. Customer benefits: what customer requirements does this Blue Ocean Strategy project address?

38. Why have you chosen the aim you have set forth?

39. What outcome, in measureable terms, are you hoping to accomplish?

40. What is the most common tool for helping define the detail?

1.2 Stakeholder Register: Blue Ocean Strategy

41. How much influence do they have on the Blue Ocean Strategy project?

42. What & Why?

43. How will reports be created?

44. What are the major Blue Ocean Strategy project milestones requiring communications or providing communications opportunities?

45. How should employers make voices heard?

46. What opportunities exist to provide communications?

47. Who are the stakeholders?

48. Who wants to talk about Security?

49. Is your organization ready for change?

50. How big is the gap?

51. Who is managing stakeholder engagement?

52. What is the power of the stakeholder?

1.3 Stakeholder Analysis Matrix: Blue Ocean Strategy

53. What is your Risk Management?

54. What tools would help you communicate?

55. Benefit to whom?

56. Why involve the stakeholder?

57. What advantages do your organizations stakeholders have?

58. New markets, vertical, horizontal?

59. Who will be affected by the work?

60. Sustaining internal capabilities?

61. Own known vulnerabilities?

62. What do people from other organizations see as your organizations weaknesses?

63. Contributions to policy and practice?

64. What mechanisms are proposed to monitor and measure Blue Ocean Strategy project performance in terms of social development outcomes?

65. What are the key services, contractual arrangements, or other relationships between

stakeholder groups?

66. How do customers express needs?

67. What is the stakeholders power and status in relation to the Blue Ocean Strategy project?

68. Are you working on the right risks?

69. Who has not been involved up to now and should have been?

70. What do you Evaluate?

71. Who influences whom?

72. What are innovative aspects of your organization?

2.0 Planning Process Group: Blue Ocean Strategy

73. What will you do to minimize the impact should a risk event occur?

74. How will you do it?

75. Have operating capacities been created and/or reinforced in partners?

76. Explanation: is what the Blue Ocean Strategy project intents to solve a hard question?

77. Have more efficient (sensitive) and appropriate measures been adopted to respond to the political and socio-cultural problems identified?

78. Did you read it correctly?

79. When developing the estimates for Blue Ocean Strategy project phases, you choose to add the individual estimates for the activities that comprise each phase. What type of estimation method are you using?

80. Is the pace of implementing the products of the program ensuring the completeness of the results of the Blue Ocean Strategy project?

81. Does it make any difference if you are successful?

82. Will the products created live up to the necessary

quality?

83. Does the program have follow-up mechanisms (to verify the quality of the products, punctuality of delivery, etc.) to measure progress in the achievement of the envisaged results?

84. Is the duration of the program sufficient to ensure a cycle that will Blue Ocean Strategy project the sustainability of the interventions?

85. How do you integrate Blue Ocean Strategy project Planning with the Iterative/Evolutionary SDLC?

86. Is your organization showing technical capacity and leadership commitment to keep working with the Blue Ocean Strategy project and to repeat it?

87. If you are late, will anybody notice?

88. What should you do next?

89. Is the schedule for the set products being met?

90. To what extent have the target population and participants made the activities own, taking an active role in it?

91. How well do the team follow the chosen processes?

2.1 Project Management Plan: Blue Ocean Strategy

92. Who is the sponsor?

93. Is mitigation authorized or recommended?

94. What is the business need?

95. When is the Blue Ocean Strategy project management plan created?

96. Do there need to be organizational changes?

97. Are there any client staffing expectations?

98. What are the deliverables?

99. Has the selected plan been formulated using cost effectiveness and incremental analysis techniques?

100. What would you do differently?

101. What went right?

102. What if, for example, the positive direction and vision of your organization causes expected trends to change resulting in greater need than expected?

103. What should you drop in order to add something new?

104. Is the engineering content at a feasibility level-

of-detail, and is it sufficiently complete, to provide an adequate basis for the baseline cost estimate?

105. How do you manage integration?

106. If the Blue Ocean Strategy project is complex or scope is specialized, do you have appropriate and/or qualified staff available to perform the tasks?

107. Does the implementation plan have an appropriate division of responsibilities?

108. Are there non-structural buyout or relocation recommendations?

109. What worked well?

110. Where does all this information come from?

2.2 Scope Management Plan: Blue Ocean Strategy

111. Is the steering committee active in Blue Ocean Strategy project oversight?

112. Is there an on-going process in place to monitor Blue Ocean Strategy project risks?

113. Have Blue Ocean Strategy project success criteria been defined?

114. Are metrics used to evaluate and manage Vendors?

115. Are action items captured and managed?

116. Alignment to strategic goals & objectives?

117. Organizational policies that might affect the availability of resources?

118. Has the Blue Ocean Strategy project manager been identified?

119. What are the risks that could significantly affect procuring consultant staff for the Blue Ocean Strategy project?

120. Pop quiz – which are the same inputs as in scope planning?

121. Quality standards - are controls in place to ensure

that the work was not only completed and also completed to meet specific standards?

122. How difficult will it be to do specific activities on this Blue Ocean Strategy project?

123. Have external dependencies been captured in the schedule?

124. What are the Quality Assurance overheads?

125. Is there a Steering Committee in place?

126. Has your organization readiness assessment been conducted?

127. Has a Blue Ocean Strategy project Communications Plan been developed?

128. Do all stakeholders know how to access this repository and where to find the Blue Ocean Strategy project documentation?

129. Was the scope definition used in task sequencing?

2.3 Requirements Management Plan: Blue Ocean Strategy

130. Is it new or replacing an existing business system or process?

131. Is infrastructure setup part of your Blue Ocean Strategy project?

132. How often will the reporting occur?

133. Did you get proper approvals?

134. Is requirements work dependent on any other specific Blue Ocean Strategy project or non-Blue Ocean Strategy project activities (e.g. funding, approvals, procurement)?

135. Will you perform a Requirements Risk assessment and develop a plan to deal with risks?

136. Will you use tracing to help understand the impact of a change in requirements?

137. In case of software development; Should you have a test for each code module?

138. How do you know that you have done this right?

139. How will you develop the schedule of requirements activities?

140. Who came up with this requirement?

141. Who will initially review the Blue Ocean Strategy project work or products to ensure it meets the applicable acceptance criteria?

142. Could inaccurate or incomplete requirements in this Blue Ocean Strategy project create a serious risk for the business?

143. How knowledgeable is the primary Stakeholder(s) in the proposed application area?

144. How will bidders price evaluations be done, by deliverables, phases, or in a big bang?

145. Do you have an appropriate arrangement for meetings?

146. Are actual resource expenditures versus planned still acceptable?

147. How detailed should the Blue Ocean Strategy project get?

148. Are all the stakeholders ready for the transition into the user community?

149. How will the information be distributed?

2.4 Requirements Documentation: Blue Ocean Strategy

150. How do you know when a Requirement is accurate enough?

151. What can tools do for us?

152. What is effective documentation?

153. How will requirements be documented and who signs off on them?

154. Has requirements gathering uncovered information that would necessitate changes?

155. Are all functions required by the customer included?

156. What images does it conjure?

157. Where do you define what is a customer, what are the attributes of customer?

158. Does your organization restrict technical alternatives?

159. Who provides requirements?

160. How will they be documented / shared?

161. Is your business case still valid?

162. Can you check system requirements?

163. What is your Elevator Speech?

164. How does what is being described meet the business need?

165. Completeness. are all functions required by the customer included?

166. Do your constraints stand?

167. Validity. does the system provide the functions which best support the customers needs?

168. What is the risk associated with cost and schedule?

169. What facilities must be supported by the system?

2.5 Requirements Traceability Matrix: Blue Ocean Strategy

170. What percentage of Blue Ocean Strategy projects are producing traceability matrices between requirements and other work products?

171. Why do you manage scope?

172. What are the chronologies, contingencies, consequences, criteria?

173. How small is small enough?

174. What is the WBS?

175. How do you manage scope?

176. Do you have a clear understanding of all subcontracts in place?

177. Is there a requirements traceability process in place?

178. Will you use a Requirements Traceability Matrix?

179. How will it affect the stakeholders personally in their career?

180. Describe the process for approving requirements so they can be added to the traceability matrix and Blue Ocean Strategy project work can be performed. Will the Blue Ocean Strategy project requirements

become approved in writing?

181. Why use a WBS?

2.6 Project Scope Statement: Blue Ocean Strategy

182. What actions will be taken to mitigate the risk?

183. Is your organization structure appropriate for the Blue Ocean Strategy projects size and complexity?

184. Will tasks be marked complete only after QA has been successfully completed?

185. Will statistics related to QA be collected, trends analyzed, and problems raised as issues?

186. What process would you recommend for creating the Blue Ocean Strategy project scope statement?

187. How will you verify the accuracy of the work of the Blue Ocean Strategy project, and what constitutes acceptance of the deliverables?

188. Is the change control process documented and on file?

189. Risks?

190. Are there backup strategies for key members of the Blue Ocean Strategy project?

191. Will this process be communicated to the customer and Blue Ocean Strategy project team?

192. Why do you need to manage scope?

193. Will the Blue Ocean Strategy project risks be managed according to the Blue Ocean Strategy projects risk management process?

194. Will the risk documents be filed?

195. Have you been able to thoroughly document the Blue Ocean Strategy projects assumptions and constraints?

196. Any new risks introduced or old risks impacted. Are there issues that could affect the existing requirements for the result, service, or product if the scope changes?

197. Blue Ocean Strategy project lead, team lead, solution architect?

198. If there are vendors, have they signed off on the Blue Ocean Strategy project Plan?

199. Did your Blue Ocean Strategy project ask for this?

200. Was planning completed before the Blue Ocean Strategy project was initiated?

2.7 Assumption and Constraint Log: Blue Ocean Strategy

201. Are requirements management tracking tools and procedures in place?

202. Is the amount of effort justified by the anticipated value of forming a new process?

203. Are there processes in place to ensure internal consistency between the source code components?

204. Were the system requirements formally reviewed prior to initiating the design phase?

205. What does an audit system look like?

206. Have all involved stakeholders and work groups committed to the Blue Ocean Strategy project?

207. Is the steering committee active in Blue Ocean Strategy project oversight?

208. Are there ways to reduce the time it takes to get something approved?

209. What weaknesses do you have?

210. How can constraints be violated?

211. Contradictory information between document sections?

212. Have all stakeholders been identified?

213. Are there nonconformance issues?

214. Does the plan conform to standards?

215. Model-building: what data-analytic strategies are useful when building proportional-hazards models?

216. Are there procedures in place to effectively manage interdependencies with other Blue Ocean Strategy projects / systems?

217. How many Blue Ocean Strategy project staff does this specific process affect?

218. Does the Blue Ocean Strategy project have a formal Blue Ocean Strategy project Plan?

219. How can you prevent/fix violations?

220. What do you audit?

2.8 Work Breakdown Structure: Blue Ocean Strategy

221. What is the probability of completing the Blue Ocean Strategy project in less that xx days?

222. Can you make it?

223. When do you stop?

224. Who has to do it?

225. What has to be done?

226. Why is it useful?

227. When does it have to be done?

228. How much detail?

229. How will you and your Blue Ocean Strategy project team define the Blue Ocean Strategy projects scope and work breakdown structure?

230. Is the work breakdown structure (wbs) defined and is the scope of the Blue Ocean Strategy project clear with assigned deliverable owners?

231. How big is a work-package?

232. When would you develop a Work Breakdown Structure?

233. Where does it take place?

234. Is it a change in scope?

235. Do you need another level?

236. What is the probability that the Blue Ocean Strategy project duration will exceed xx weeks?

237. Why would you develop a Work Breakdown Structure?

238. How many levels?

239. Is it still viable?

240. How far down?

2.9 WBS Dictionary: Blue Ocean Strategy

241. Are records maintained to show full accountability for all material purchased for the contract, including the residual inventory?

242. Are the latest revised estimates of costs at completion compared with the established budgets at appropriate levels and causes of variances identified?

243. Major functional areas of contract effort?

244. Does the contractors system provide for determination of price variance by comparing planned Vs actual commitments?

245. Is the entire contract planned in time-phased control accounts to the extent practicable?

246. The already stated responsible for overhead performance control of related costs?

247. Does the contractors system provide for the determination of cost variances attributable to the excess usage of material?

248. Are retroactive changes to direct costs and indirect costs prohibited except for the correction of errors and routine accounting adjustments?

249. Should you include sub-activities?

250. Are overhead costs budgets established on a basis consistent with anticipated direct business base?

251. Are the bases and rates for allocating costs from each indirect pool to commercial work consistent with the already stated used to allocate corresponding costs to Government contracts?

252. Does the contractors system provide unit or lot costs when applicable?

253. Are work packages assigned to performing organizations?

254. Are detailed work packages planned as far in advance as practicable?

255. Is the anticipated (firm and potential) business base Blue Ocean Strategy projected in a rational, consistent manner?

256. Is work progressively subdivided into detailed work packages as requirements are defined?

257. Are material costs reported within the same period as that in which BCWP is earned for that material?

258. Do work packages consist of discrete tasks which are adequately described?

259. All cwbs elements specified for external reporting?

260. Is budgeted cost for work performed calculated in a manner consistent with the way work is planned?

2.10 Schedule Management Plan: Blue Ocean Strategy

261. Is current scope of the Blue Ocean Strategy project substantially different than that originally defined?

262. Are adequate resources provided for the quality assurance function?

263. Are non-critical path items updated and agreed upon with the teams?

264. Can additional resources be added to subsequent tasks to reduce the durations of the already stated tasks?

265. Is the development plan and/or process documented?

266. Has a sponsor been identified?

267. Must the Blue Ocean Strategy project be complete by a specified date?

268. Is a process defined to measure the performance of the schedule management process itself?

269. Has a quality assurance plan been developed for the Blue Ocean Strategy project?

270. Is there an on-going process in place to monitor Blue Ocean Strategy project risks?

271. Are the Blue Ocean Strategy project team members located locally to the users/stakeholders?

272. Are scheduled deliverables actually delivered?

273. Is there a requirements change management processes in place?

274. Are written status reports provided on a designated frequent basis?

275. Has the Blue Ocean Strategy project manager been identified?

276. Were Blue Ocean Strategy project team members involved in detailed estimating and scheduling?

277. Have Blue Ocean Strategy project success criteria been defined?

278. Is the critical path valid?

279. Are internal Blue Ocean Strategy project status meetings held at reasonable intervals?

280. How relevant is this attribute to this Blue Ocean Strategy project or audit?

2.11 Activity List: Blue Ocean Strategy

281. What went wrong?

282. What did not go as well?

283. Is there anything planned that does not need to be here?

284. What is the LF and LS for each activity?

285. What is the total time required to complete the Blue Ocean Strategy project if no delays occur?

286. What are the critical bottleneck activities?

287. For other activities, how much delay can be tolerated?

288. When do the individual activities need to start and finish?

289. How can the Blue Ocean Strategy project be displayed graphically to better visualize the activities?

290. What is your organizations history in doing similar activities?

291. How difficult will it be to do specific activities on this Blue Ocean Strategy project?

292. Is infrastructure setup part of your Blue Ocean Strategy project?

293. How detailed should a Blue Ocean Strategy project get?

294. Can you determine the activity that must finish, before this activity can start?

295. How do you determine the late start (LS) for each activity?

296. In what sequence?

297. What are you counting on?

298. How should ongoing costs be monitored to try to keep the Blue Ocean Strategy project within budget?

299. Are the required resources available or need to be acquired?

2.12 Activity Attributes: Blue Ocean Strategy

300. Why?

301. Activity: what is In the Bag?

302. Activity: fair or not fair?

303. How much activity detail is required?

304. How else could the items be grouped?

305. Can you re-assign any activities to another resource to resolve an over-allocation?

306. Were there other ways you could have organized the data to achieve similar results?

307. Where else does it apply?

308. How many resources do you need to complete the work scope within a limit of X number of days?

309. Activity: what is Missing?

310. How difficult will it be to complete specific activities on this Blue Ocean Strategy project?

311. What activity do you think you should spend the most time on?

312. What is the general pattern here?

313. Is there a trend during the year?

314. Time for overtime?

2.13 Milestone List: Blue Ocean Strategy

315. What has been done so far?

316. Environmental effects?

317. Competitive advantages?

318. What background experience, skills, and strengths does the team bring to your organization?

319. Global influences?

320. How late can each activity be finished and started?

321. How do you manage time?

322. Who will manage the Blue Ocean Strategy project on a day-to-day basis?

323. How difficult will it be to do specific activities on this Blue Ocean Strategy project?

324. Gaps in capabilities?

325. What specific improvements did you make to the Blue Ocean Strategy project proposal since the previous time?

326. Which path is the critical path?

327. Reliability of data, plan predictability?

328. Calculate how long can activity be delayed?

329. How late can the activity start?

330. Usps (unique selling points)?

331. Legislative effects?

332. Describe the concept of the technology, product or service that will be or has been developed. How will it be used?

2.14 Network Diagram: Blue Ocean Strategy

333. What job or jobs could run concurrently?

334. What to do and When?

335. What job or jobs follow it?

336. If x is long, what would be the completion time if you break x into two parallel parts of y weeks and z weeks?

337. If the Blue Ocean Strategy project network diagram cannot change and you have extra personnel resources, what is the BEST thing to do?

338. What is the lowest cost to complete this Blue Ocean Strategy project in xx weeks?

339. What must be completed before an activity can be started?

340. What are the Key Success Factors?

341. Where do schedules come from?

342. What is the completion time?

343. Planning: who, how long, what to do?

344. Are the required resources available?

345. What activity must be completed immediately before this activity can start?

346. Are you on time?

347. Are the gantt chart and/or network diagram updated periodically and used to assess the overall Blue Ocean Strategy project timetable?

348. What activities must occur simultaneously with this activity?

349. Where do you schedule uncertainty time?

350. Review the logical flow of the network diagram. Take a look at which activities you have first and then sequence the activities. Do they make sense?

351. Why must you schedule milestones, such as reviews, throughout the Blue Ocean Strategy project?

2.15 Activity Resource Requirements: Blue Ocean Strategy

352. Are there unresolved issues that need to be addressed?

353. Other support in specific areas?

354. Anything else?

355. Which logical relationship does the PDM use most often?

356. Do you use tools like decomposition and rolling-wave planning to produce the activity list and other outputs?

357. What is the Work Plan Standard?

358. How many signatures do you require on a check and does this match what is in your policy and procedures?

359. What are constraints that you might find during the Human Resource Planning process?

360. How do you handle petty cash?

361. Organizational Applicability?

362. Why do you do that?

363. When does monitoring begin?

2.16 Resource Breakdown Structure: Blue Ocean Strategy

364. Which resources should be in the resource pool?

365. Who is allowed to see what data about which resources?

366. What is each stakeholders desired outcome for the Blue Ocean Strategy project?

367. Who delivers the information?

368. Which resource planning tool provides information on resource responsibility and accountability?

369. Why time management?

370. What is the purpose of assigning and documenting responsibility?

371. What is Blue Ocean Strategy project communication management?

372. The list could probably go on, but, the thing that you would most like to know is, How long & How much?

373. What is the difference between % Complete and % work?

374. Any changes from stakeholders?

375. What is the number one predictor of a groups productivity?

376. Who will use the system?

377. What is the primary purpose of the human resource plan?

378. How difficult will it be to do specific activities on this Blue Ocean Strategy project?

379. Who is allowed to perform which functions?

380. How should the information be delivered?

2.17 Activity Duration Estimates: Blue Ocean Strategy

381. After changes are approved are Blue Ocean Strategy project documents updated and distributed?

382. How could you define throughput and how would your organization benefit from maximizing it?

383. Research recruiting and retention strategies at three different companies. What distinguishes one organization from another in this area?

384. Consider the changes in the job market for information technology workers. How does the job market and current state of the economy affect human resource management?

385. Under corresponding circumstances what would be the best thing to do?

386. How can others help Blue Ocean Strategy project managers understand your organizational context for Blue Ocean Strategy projects?

387. What tasks must precede this task?

388. How can software assist in Blue Ocean Strategy project communications?

389. What are the options you found to help people prepare for the exam?

390. What is pmp certification, and why do you think the number of people earning it has grown so much in the past ten years?

391. Are Blue Ocean Strategy project results verified and Blue Ocean Strategy project documents archived?

392. Why is activity definition the first process involved in Blue Ocean Strategy project time management?

393. Which type of mathematical analysis is being used?

394. Calculate the expected duration for an activity that has a most likely time of 5, a pessimistic time of 13, and a optimiztic time of 3?

395. What are the largest companies that provide information technology outsourcing services?

396. Does a process exist to determine the potential loss or gain if risk events occur?

397. Are tools and techniques defined for gathering, integrating and distributing Blue Ocean Strategy project outputs?

398. Are risks that are likely to affect the Blue Ocean Strategy project identified and documented?

399. On which process should team members spend the most time?

400. Is a standard form used to obtain bids and proposals from prospective sellers?

2.18 Duration Estimating Worksheet: Blue Ocean Strategy

401. What is your role?

402. What work will be included in the Blue Ocean Strategy project?

403. Science = process: remember the scientific method?

404. How should ongoing costs be monitored to try to keep the Blue Ocean Strategy project within budget?

405. Is a construction detail attached (to aid in explanation)?

406. Is the Blue Ocean Strategy project responsive to community need?

407. Done before proceeding with this activity or what can be done concurrently?

408. What is the total time required to complete the Blue Ocean Strategy project if no delays occur?

409. What info is needed?

410. Is this operation cost effective?

411. Define the work as completely as possible. What work will be included in the Blue Ocean Strategy project?

412. Value pocket identification & quantification what are value pockets?

413. What utility impacts are there?

414. Can the Blue Ocean Strategy project be constructed as planned?

415. What is an Average Blue Ocean Strategy project?

2.19 Project Schedule: Blue Ocean Strategy

416. Is the structure for tracking the Blue Ocean Strategy project schedule well defined and assigned to a specific individual?

417. How does a Blue Ocean Strategy project get to be a year late ?

418. How can you shorten the schedule?

419. Did the Blue Ocean Strategy project come in under budget?

420. Why do you need schedules?

421. Does the condition or event threaten the Blue Ocean Strategy projects objectives in any ways?

422. Your best shot for providing estimations how complex/how much work does the activity require?

423. Why do you think schedule issues often cause the most conflicts on Blue Ocean Strategy projects?

424. How much slack is available in the Blue Ocean Strategy project?

425. How do you manage Blue Ocean Strategy project Risk?

426. Are there activities that came from a template

or previous Blue Ocean Strategy project that are not applicable on this phase of this Blue Ocean Strategy project?

427. What is risk?

428. Schedule/cost recovery?

429. Are key risk mitigation strategies added to the Blue Ocean Strategy project schedule?

430. Is infrastructure setup part of your Blue Ocean Strategy project?

431. Are all remaining durations correct?

432. Are the original Blue Ocean Strategy project schedule and budget realistic?

433. How can you fix it?

2.20 Cost Management Plan: Blue Ocean Strategy

434. Are the quality tools and methods identified in the Quality Plan appropriate to the Blue Ocean Strategy project?

435. Are Blue Ocean Strategy project team members committed fulltime?

436. Has a provision been made to reassess Blue Ocean Strategy project risks at various Blue Ocean Strategy project stages?

437. Have the key functions and capabilities been defined and assigned to each release or iteration?

438. Were the budget estimates reasonable?

439. Owner, contractor, and subcontractors?

440. Have process improvement efforts been completed before requirements efforts begin?

441. Schedule variances – how will schedule variances be identified and corrected?

442. Is the communication plan being followed?

443. Are the results of quality assurance reviews provided to affected groups & individuals?

444. Are issues raised, assessed, actioned, and

resolved in a timely and efficient manner?

445. Have all documents been archived in a Blue Ocean Strategy project repository for each release?

446. Has the schedule been baselined?

447. Published materials?

448. Cost / benefit analysis?

449. What are the Blue Ocean Strategy project objectives?

450. Are estimating assumptions and constraints captured?

451. Were Blue Ocean Strategy project team members involved in detailed estimating and scheduling?

452. Contracting method – what contracting method is to be used for the contracts?

2.21 Activity Cost Estimates: Blue Ocean Strategy

453. Were you satisfied with the work?

454. Was it performed on time?

455. What is included in indirect cost being allocated?

456. Does the activity serve a common type of customer?

457. Were the costs or charges reasonable?

458. Who determines when the contractor is paid?

459. Review – what are some common errors in activities to avoid?

460. Where can you get activity reports?

461. Measurable - are the targets measurable?

462. Specific - is the objective clear in terms of what, how, when, and where the situation will be changed?

463. Which contract type places the most risk on the seller?

464. Will you use any tools, such as Blue Ocean Strategy project management software, to assist in capturing Earned Value metrics?

465. What were things that you did well, and could improve, and how?

466. Was the consultant knowledgeable about the program?

467. What are you looking for?

468. What skill level is required to do the job?

469. How and when do you enter into Blue Ocean Strategy project Procurement Management?

470. What makes a good expected result statement?

471. What is the activity recast of the budget?

472. In which phase of the acquisition process cycle does source qualifications reside?

2.22 Cost Estimating Worksheet: Blue Ocean Strategy

473. Can a trend be established from historical performance data on the selected measure and are the criteria for using trend analysis or forecasting methods met?

474. Is the Blue Ocean Strategy project responsive to community need?

475. Identify the timeframe necessary to monitor progress and collect data to determine how the selected measure has changed?

476. What will others want?

477. What is the estimated labor cost today based upon this information?

478. Will the Blue Ocean Strategy project collaborate with the local community and leverage resources?

479. What happens to any remaining funds not used?

480. Is it feasible to establish a control group arrangement?

481. How will the results be shared and to whom?

482. What additional Blue Ocean Strategy project(s) could be initiated as a result of this Blue Ocean Strategy project?

483. Who is best positioned to know and assist in identifying corresponding factors?

484. What can be included?

485. What costs are to be estimated?

486. What is the purpose of estimating?

487. Does the Blue Ocean Strategy project provide innovative ways for stakeholders to overcome obstacles or deliver better outcomes?

488. Ask: are others positioned to know, are others credible, and will others cooperate?

2.23 Cost Baseline: Blue Ocean Strategy

489. What does a good WBS NOT look like?

490. On budget?

491. Have all the product or service deliverables been accepted by the customer?

492. Are you asking management for something as a result of this update?

493. Has the Blue Ocean Strategy project documentation been archived or otherwise disposed as described in the Blue Ocean Strategy project communication plan?

494. Have you identified skills that are missing from your team?

495. How difficult will it be to do specific tasks on the Blue Ocean Strategy project?

496. Are procedures defined by which the cost baseline may be changed?

497. What is your organizations history in doing similar tasks?

498. Have all approved changes to the cost baseline been identified and impact on the Blue Ocean Strategy project documented?

499. Is there anything you need from upper management in order to be successful?

500. Who will use corresponding metrics ?

501. Does it impact schedule, cost, quality?

502. How will cost estimates be used?

503. How do you manage cost?

504. When should cost estimates be developed?

505. What would the life cycle costs be?

506. What can go wrong?

507. Should a more thorough impact analysis be conducted?

2.24 Quality Management Plan: Blue Ocean Strategy

508. How do you manage quality?

509. How are calibration records kept?

510. Results Available?

511. How are corresponding standards measured?

512. Can the requirements be traced to the appropriate components of the solution, as well as test scripts?

513. How does your organization ensure the reliability, accuracy, timeliness, security and accessibility of data and information?

514. Meet how often?

515. Do trained quality assurance auditors conduct the audits as defined in the Quality Management Plan and scheduled by the Blue Ocean Strategy project manager?

516. What is the Difference Between a QMP and QAPP?

517. Sampling part of task?

518. Can you perform this task or activity in a more effective manner?

519. What are your organizations current levels and trends for the already stated measures related to customer satisfaction/ dissatisfaction and product/ service performance?

520. How are changes recorded?

521. How does your organization use comparative data and information to improve organizational performance?

522. How do you field-modify testing procedures?

523. How are changes approved?

524. What is your organizations strategic planning process?

525. Has a Blue Ocean Strategy project Communications Plan been developed?

2.25 Quality Metrics: Blue Ocean Strategy

526. When will the Final Guidance will be issued?

527. How can the effectiveness of each of the activities be measured?

528. How exactly do you define when differences exist?

529. Are documents on hand to provide explanations of privacy and confidentiality?

530. Did evaluation start on time?

531. Have alternatives been defined in the event that failure occurs?

532. Were quality attributes reported?

533. Has it met internal or external standards?

534. Have risk areas been identified?

535. How do you communicate results and findings to upper management?

536. How effective are your security tests?

537. What is the benchmark?

538. What group is empowered to define quality

requirements?

539. When is the security analysis testing complete?

540. Which data do others need in one place to target areas of improvement?

541. Was review conducted per standard protocols?

542. There are many reasons to shore up quality-related metrics, and what metrics are important?

543. How does one achieve stability?

544. Where did complaints, returns and warranty claims come from?

545. Was material distributed on time?

2.26 Process Improvement Plan: Blue Ocean Strategy

546. To elicit goal statements, do you ask a question such as, What do you want to achieve?

547. What personnel are the coaches for your initiative?

548. Are you making progress on the goals?

549. Are you making progress on the improvement framework?

550. Are there forms and procedures to collect and record the data?

551. Purpose of goal: the motive is determined by asking, why do you want to achieve this goal?

552. What personnel are the change agents for your initiative?

553. What personnel are the champions for the initiative?

554. What makes people good SPI coaches?

555. Does your process ensure quality?

556. Who should prepare the process improvement action plan?

557. Has the time line required to move measurement results from the points of collection to databases or users been established?

558. What is the return on investment?

559. Where do you focus?

560. Does explicit definition of the measures exist?

561. Has a process guide to collect the data been developed?

562. Why do you want to achieve the goal?

563. Are you meeting the quality standards?

564. Modeling current processes is great, and will you ever see a return on that investment?

565. Have the supporting tools been developed or acquired?

2.27 Responsibility Assignment Matrix: Blue Ocean Strategy

566. Does the scheduling system identify in a timely manner the status of work?

567. Budgets assigned to major functional organizations?

568. Will too many Signing-off responsibilities delay the completion of the activity/deliverable?

569. Direct labor dollars and/or hours?

570. Does the accounting system provide a basis for auditing records of direct costs chargeable to the contract?

571. What can you do to improve productivity?

572. Are the bases and rates for allocating costs from each indirect pool consistently applied?

573. Can the contractor substantiate work package and planning package budgets?

574. Are the requirements for all items of overhead established by rational, traceable processes?

575. Are the actual costs used for variance analysis reconcilable with data from the accounting system?

576. Are management actions taken to reduce

indirect costs when there are significant adverse variances?

577. Not any rs, as, or cs: if an identified role is only informed, should others be eliminated from the matrix?

578. Do all the identified groups or people really need to be consulted?

579. Undistributed budgets, if any?

580. Are indirect costs accumulated for comparison with the corresponding budgets?

581. Is data disseminated to the contractors management timely, accurate, and usable?

582. Does the Blue Ocean Strategy project need to be analyzed further to uncover additional responsibilities?

583. How do you manage human resources?

2.28 Roles and Responsibilities: Blue Ocean Strategy

584. Are your budgets supportive of a culture of quality data?

585. Who is responsible for implementation activities and where will the functions, roles and responsibilities be defined?

586. Have you ever been a part of this team?

587. Concern: where are you limited or have no authority, where you can not influence?

588. Once the responsibilities are defined for the Blue Ocean Strategy project, have the deliverables, roles and responsibilities been clearly communicated to every participant?

589. Are Blue Ocean Strategy project team roles and responsibilities identified and documented?

590. What is working well?

591. Required skills, knowledge, experience?

592. Are Blue Ocean Strategy project team roles and responsibilities identified and documented?

593. Attainable / achievable: the goal is attainable; can you actually accomplish the goal?

594. Are your policies supportive of a culture of quality data?

595. Does your vision/mission support a culture of quality data?

596. Where are you most strong as a supervisor?

597. Authority: what areas/Blue Ocean Strategy projects in your work do you have the authority to decide upon and act on the already stated decisions?

598. What is working well within your organizations performance management system?

599. What are your major roles and responsibilities in the area of performance measurement and assessment?

600. What specific behaviors did you observe?

601. Once the responsibilities are defined for the Blue Ocean Strategy project, have the deliverables, roles and responsibilities been clearly communicated to every participant?

602. What expectations were met?

603. Was the expectation clearly communicated?

2.29 Human Resource Management Plan: Blue Ocean Strategy

604. Has a Blue Ocean Strategy project Communications Plan been developed?

605. Quality assurance overheads?

606. Are risk oriented checklists used during risk identification?

607. Does a documented Blue Ocean Strategy project organizational policy & plan (i.e. governance model) exist?

608. Have reserves been created to address risks?

609. Are decisions captured in a decisions log?

610. Is it possible to track all classes of Blue Ocean Strategy project work (e.g. scheduled, un-scheduled, defect repair, etc.)?

611. Does the detailed work plan match the complexity of tasks with the capabilities of personnel?

612. Are trade-offs between accepting the risk and mitigating the risk identified?

613. Are software metrics formally captured, analyzed and used as a basis for other Blue Ocean Strategy project estimates?

614. Sensitivity analysis?

615. How do you determine what key skills and talents are needed to meet the objectives. Is your organization primarily focused on a specific industry?

616. What did you have to assume to be true to complete the charter?

617. Has a quality assurance plan been developed for the Blue Ocean Strategy project?

618. Does all Blue Ocean Strategy project documentation reside in a common repository for easy access?

619. Are quality metrics defined?

620. Is quality monitored from the perspective of the customers needs and expectations?

621. What talent is needed?

622. Were sponsors and decision makers available when needed outside regularly scheduled meetings?

623. Is there a formal set of procedures supporting Issues Management?

2.30 Communications Management Plan: Blue Ocean Strategy

624. Are you constantly rushing from meeting to meeting?

625. What communications method?

626. Timing: when do the effects of the communication take place?

627. Where do team members get information?

628. What is Blue Ocean Strategy project communications management?

629. What steps can you take for a positive relationship?

630. What approaches do you use?

631. Who have you worked with in past, similar initiatives?

632. What to know?

633. Will messages be directly related to the release strategy or phases of the Blue Ocean Strategy project?

634. Do you prepare stakeholder engagement plans?

635. Is there an important stakeholder who is actively opposed and will not receive messages?

636. Is the stakeholder role recognized by your organization?

637. What is the political influence?

638. Who did you turn to if you had questions?

639. Are stakeholders internal or external?

640. What does the stakeholder need from the team?

641. Who is responsible?

642. Which stakeholders are thought leaders, influences, or early adopters?

2.31 Risk Management Plan: Blue Ocean Strategy

643. Costs associated with late delivery or a defective product?

644. Minimize cost and financial risk?

645. What will drive change?

646. Anticipated volatility of the requirements?

647. Are tool mentors available?

648. Is the necessary data being captured and is it complete and accurate?

649. Is the process being followed?

650. Which is an input to the risk management process?

651. For software; are compilers and code generators available and suitable for the product to be built?

652. Who/what can assist?

653. Risks should be identified during which phase of Blue Ocean Strategy project management life cycle?

654. Are end-users enthusiastically committed to the Blue Ocean Strategy project and the system/product to be built?

655. Are there new risks that mitigation strategies might introduce?

656. Do you train all developers in the process?

657. What risks are tracked?

658. Mitigation -how can you avoid the risk?

659. How risk averse are you?

660. User involvement: do you have the right users?

661. How much risk can you tolerate?

2.32 Risk Register: Blue Ocean Strategy

662. What action, if any, has been taken to respond to the risk?

663. Why would you develop a risk register?

664. Preventative actions - planned actions to reduce the likelihood a risk will occur and/or reduce the seriousness should it occur. What should you do now?

665. Having taken action, how did the responses effect change, and where is the Blue Ocean Strategy project now?

666. Do you require further engagement?

667. Assume the risk event or situation happens, what would the impact be?

668. Are there other alternative controls that could be implemented?

669. Does the evidence highlight any areas to advance opportunities or foster good relations. If yes what steps will be taken?

670. Technology risk -is the Blue Ocean Strategy project technically feasible?

671. What are the assumptions and current status that support the assessment of the risk?

672. Assume the event happens, what is the Most Likely impact?

673. Risk documentation: what reporting formats and processes will be used for risk management activities?

674. When will it happen?

675. Cost/benefit – how much will the proposed mitigations cost and how does this cost compare with the potential cost of the risk event/situation should it occur?

676. What has changed since the last period?

677. How are risks graded?

678. What should you do when?

679. When would you develop a risk register?

680. Financial risk -can your organization afford to undertake the Blue Ocean Strategy project?

681. What can be done about it?

2.33 Probability and Impact Assessment: Blue Ocean Strategy

682. Who will be in command to monitor and control the performance of the consortium members (consortium leader/client)?

683. Who has experience with this?

684. Monitoring of the overall Blue Ocean Strategy project status – are there any changes in the Blue Ocean Strategy project that can effect and cause new possible risks?

685. Do benefits and chances of success outweigh potential damage if success is not attained?

686. Are the risk data complete?

687. How solid is the Blue Ocean Strategy projection of competitive reaction?

688. To what extent is the chosen technology maturing?

689. What are the likely future requirements?

690. Is the Blue Ocean Strategy project cutting across the entire organization?

691. What should be the level of difficulty in handling the technology?

692. Will new information become available during the Blue Ocean Strategy project?

693. How would you suggest monitoring for risk transition indicators?

694. What should be the external organizations responsibility vis-à-vis total stake in the Blue Ocean Strategy project?

695. How is the risk management process used in practice?

696. Are the software tools integrated with each other?

697. How completely has the customer been identified?

698. What is the likely future demand of the customer?

699. Can you avoid altogether some things that might go wrong?

700. How well is the risk understood?

2.34 Probability and Impact Matrix: Blue Ocean Strategy

701. Brain storm – mind maps, what if?

702. What can you use the analyzed risks for?

703. Do you manage the process through use of metrics?

704. What will be the impact or consequence if the risk occurs?

705. Is the customer willing to participate in reviews?

706. Do you use any methods to analyze risks?

707. What new technologies are being explored in the same area?

708. Are formal technical reviews part of this process?

709. What is the political situation at present?

710. Were there any Blue Ocean Strategy projects similar to this one in existence?

711. What are its business ethics?

712. Can you handle the investment risk?

713. What are data sources?

714. Mandated delivery date?

715. What would be the effect of slippage?

716. Is the Blue Ocean Strategy project cutting across the entire organization?

717. Do you have a mechanism for managing change?

2.35 Risk Data Sheet: Blue Ocean Strategy

718. What actions can be taken to eliminate or remove risk?

719. What will be the consequences if it happens?

720. Do effective diagnostic tests exist?

721. What were the Causes that contributed?

722. What if client refuses?

723. How reliable is the data source?

724. What is the chance that it will happen?

725. What do people affected think about the need for, and practicality of preventive measures?

726. What can happen?

727. How can hazards be reduced?

728. What is the environment within which you operate (social trends, economic, community values, broad based participation, national directions etc.)?

729. Are new hazards created?

730. What are you trying to achieve (Objectives)?

731. During work activities could hazards exist?

732. What do you know?

733. Whom do you serve (customers)?

734. What are the main opportunities available to you that you should grab while you can?

735. How do you handle product safely?

736. Who has a vested interest in how you perform as your organization (our stakeholders)?

737. How can it happen?

2.36 Procurement Management Plan: Blue Ocean Strategy

738. Are post milestone Blue Ocean Strategy project reviews (PMPR) conducted with your organization at least once a year?

739. What types of contracts will be used?

740. Are corrective actions and variances reported?

741. Have all necessary approvals been obtained?

742. Has the business need been clearly defined?

743. Are the schedule estimates reasonable given the Blue Ocean Strategy project?

744. What are things that you need to improve?

745. Has a Blue Ocean Strategy project Communications Plan been developed?

746. Have key stakeholders been identified?

747. Is there a set of procedures defining the scope, procedures, and deliverables defining quality control?

748. Has Blue Ocean Strategy project success criteria been defined?

749. Is the Blue Ocean Strategy project schedule available for all Blue Ocean Strategy project team

members to review?

750. Have all unresolved risks been documented?

751. Are there checklists created to determine if all quality processes are followed?

752. Have stakeholder accountabilities & responsibilities been clearly defined?

753. Are all payments made according to the contract(s)?

2.37 Source Selection Criteria: Blue Ocean Strategy

754. Do you consider all weaknesses, significant weaknesses, and deficiencies?

755. What should be the contracting officers strategy?

756. Have all evaluators been trained?

757. What will you use to capture evaluation and subsequent documentation?

758. What past performance information should be requested?

759. What risks were identified in the proposals?

760. Comparison of each offers prices to the estimated prices -are there significant differences?

761. What is the last item a Blue Ocean Strategy project manager must do to finalize Blue Ocean Strategy project close-out?

762. If the costs are normalized, please account for how the normalization is conducted. Is a cost realism analysis used?

763. Is the contracting office likely to receive more purchase requests for this item or service during the coming year?

764. Are responses to considerations adequate?

765. Are considerations anticipated?

766. How can solicitation Schedules be improved to yield more effective price competition?

767. Has all proposal data been loaded?

768. Can you prevent comparison of proposals?

769. Does the evaluation of any change include an impact analysis; how will the change affect the scope, time, cost, and quality of the goods or services being provided?

770. In the technical/management area, what criteria do you use to determine the final evaluation ratings?

771. How are oral presentations documented?

772. How should comments received in response to a RFP be handled?

2.38 Stakeholder Management Plan: Blue Ocean Strategy

773. Have the key elements of a coherent Blue Ocean Strategy project management strategy been established?

774. What action will be taken once reports have been received?

775. Does the system design reflect the requirements?

776. Is the quality assurance team identified?

777. Are regulatory inspections considered part of quality control?

778. Are mitigation strategies identified?

779. Are Blue Ocean Strategy project team members committed fulltime?

780. Are there any potential occupational health and safety issues due to the proposed purchases?

781. Are Blue Ocean Strategy project contact logs kept up to date?

782. How accurate and complete is the information?

783. Has a structured approach been used to break work effort into manageable components (WBS)?

784. Is staff trained on the software technologies that are being used on the Blue Ocean Strategy project?

785. Who is gathering information?

786. At what point will the Blue Ocean Strategy project be closed and what will be done to formally close the Blue Ocean Strategy project?

787. Describe the process that will be used to design, develop, review, accept, distribute and change outputs. Will all outputs delivered by the Blue Ocean Strategy project follow the same process?

788. Are there standards for code development?

2.39 Change Management Plan: Blue Ocean Strategy

789. What is going to be done differently?

790. What type of materials/channels will be available to leverage?

791. Have the approved procedures and policies been published?

792. What are the current methods of sharing information and do there need to be new ones developed?

793. What are the dependencies?

794. Has the training provider been established?

795. What is the reason for the communication?

796. How might they respond to the message and if the response may be negative or open to misinterpretation, what else needs to be said?

797. What would be an estimate of the total cost for the activities required to carry out the change initiative?

798. Is there a need for new relationships to be built?

799. What is the negative impact of communicating too soon or too late?

800. Where will the funds come from?

801. Who will fund the training?

802. When should a given message be communicated?

803. What can you do to minimise misinterpretation and negative perceptions?

804. What relationships will change?

805. How will the stakeholders share information and transfer knowledge?

806. Is there support for this application(s) and are the details available for distribution?

807. Has an information & communications plan been developed?

3.0 Executing Process Group: Blue Ocean Strategy

808. What business situation is being addressed?

809. What are some crucial elements of a good Blue Ocean Strategy project plan?

810. How does Blue Ocean Strategy project management relate to other disciplines?

811. Why do you need a good WBS to use Blue Ocean Strategy project management software?

812. How well did the chosen processes fit the needs of the Blue Ocean Strategy project?

813. It under budget or over budget?

814. How well defined and documented were the Blue Ocean Strategy project management processes you chose to use?

815. What factors are contributing to progress or delay in the achievement of products and results?

816. Would you rate yourself as being risk-averse, risk-neutral, or risk-seeking?

817. What is involved in the solicitation process?

818. Are decisions made in a timely manner?

819. How does a Blue Ocean Strategy project life cycle differ from a product life cycle?

820. How well did the team follow the chosen processes?

821. What type of information goes in the quality assurance plan?

822. Will outside resources be needed to help?

823. What are the critical steps involved with strategy mapping?

3.1 Team Member Status Report: Blue Ocean Strategy

824. How will resource planning be done?

825. What is to be done?

826. How does this product, good, or service meet the needs of the Blue Ocean Strategy project and your organization as a whole?

827. Do you have an Enterprise Blue Ocean Strategy project Management Office (EPMO)?

828. Are the attitudes of staff regarding Blue Ocean Strategy project work improving?

829. Are your organizations Blue Ocean Strategy projects more successful over time?

830. Will the staff do training or is that done by a third party?

831. Does every department have to have a Blue Ocean Strategy project Manager on staff?

832. The problem with Reward & Recognition Programs is that the truly deserving people all too often get left out. How can you make it practical?

833. Does the product, good, or service already exist within your organization?

834. How can you make it practical?

835. How much risk is involved?

836. What specific interest groups do you have in place?

837. When a teams productivity and success depend on collaboration and the efficient flow of information, what generally fails them?

838. Is there evidence that staff is taking a more professional approach toward management of your organizations Blue Ocean Strategy projects?

839. Why is it to be done?

840. Are the products of your organizations Blue Ocean Strategy projects meeting customers objectives?

841. How it is to be done?

842. Does your organization have the means (staff, money, contract, etc.) to produce or to acquire the product, good, or service?

3.2 Change Request: Blue Ocean Strategy

843. Are change requests logged and managed?

844. Who has responsibility for approving and ranking changes?

845. How shall the implementation of changes be recorded?

846. What is the purpose of change control?

847. How to get changes (code) out in a timely manner?

848. What are the duties of the change control team?

849. What is the relationship between requirements attributes and reliability?

850. When do you create a change request?

851. Who can suggest changes?

852. Who is included in the change control team?

853. Why were your requested changes rejected or not made?

854. Has your address changed?

855. Who will perform the change?

856. Can you answer what happened, who did it, when did it happen, and what else will be affected?

857. What are the requirements for urgent changes?

858. What needs to be communicated?

859. How fast will change requests be approved?

860. When to submit a change request?

861. Change request coordination ?

862. Why control change across the life cycle?

3.3 Change Log: Blue Ocean Strategy

863. How does this relate to the standards developed for specific business processes?

864. Is the submitted change a new change or a modification of a previously approved change?

865. Is the change request within Blue Ocean Strategy project scope?

866. How does this change affect scope?

867. How does this change affect the timeline of the schedule?

868. Who initiated the change request?

869. Is the requested change request a result of changes in other Blue Ocean Strategy project(s)?

870. Does the suggested change request represent a desired enhancement to the products functionality?

871. Where do changes come from?

872. When was the request submitted?

873. Does the suggested change request seem to represent a necessary enhancement to the product?

874. Is this a mandatory replacement?

875. Is the change backward compatible without

limitations?

876. When was the request approved?

877. Do the described changes impact on the integrity or security of the system?

878. Will the Blue Ocean Strategy project fail if the change request is not executed?

879. Is the change request open, closed or pending?

3.4 Decision Log: Blue Ocean Strategy

880. Which variables make a critical difference?

881. Behaviors; what are guidelines that the team has identified that will assist them with getting the most out of team meetings?

882. Meeting purpose; why does this team meet?

883. Who will be given a copy of this document and where will it be kept?

884. What makes you different or better than others companies selling the same thing?

885. What is the average size of your matters in an applicable measurement?

886. Is your opponent open to a non-traditional workflow, or will it likely challenge anything you do?

887. Does anything need to be adjusted?

888. At what point in time does loss become unacceptable?

889. What is the line where eDiscovery ends and document review begins?

890. Is everything working as expected?

891. How effective is maintaining the log at facilitating organizational learning?

892. Linked to original objective?

893. What alternatives/risks were considered?

894. Do strategies and tactics aimed at less than full control reduce the costs of management or simply shift the cost burden?

895. Decision-making process; how will the team make decisions?

896. Adversarial environment. is your opponent open to a non-traditional workflow, or will it likely challenge anything you do?

897. How do you define success?

898. With whom was the decision shared or considered?

899. It becomes critical to track and periodically revisit both operational effectiveness; Are you noticing all that you need to, and are you interpreting what you see effectively?

3.5 Quality Audit: Blue Ocean Strategy

900. How does your organization know that its methods are appropriately effective and constructive?

901. Does everyone know what they are supposed to be doing, how and why?

902. How does your organization know that its system for managing intellectual property issues is appropriately effective, constructive and fair?

903. Are training programs documented?

904. What happens if your organization fails its Quality Audit?

905. Are all employees including salespersons made aware that they must report all complaints received from any source for inclusion in the complaint handling system?

906. How does your organization know that its system for governing staff behaviour is appropriately effective and constructive?

907. How does your organization know that its staff financial services are appropriately effective and constructive?

908. What does an analysis of your organizations staff profile suggest in terms of its planning, and how is

this being addressed?

909. Is there any content that may be legally actionable?

910. Has a written procedure been established to identify devices during all stages of receipt, reconditioning, distribution and installation so that mix-ups are prevented?

911. Are all areas associated with the storage and reconditioning of devices clean, free of rubbish, adequately ventilated and in good repair?

912. How does your organization know that it provides a safe and healthy environment?

913. Is the continuing professional education of key personnel account fored in detail?

914. Are all records associated with the reconditioning of a device maintained for a minimum of two years after the sale or disposal of the last device within a lot of merchandise?

915. How does your organization know that its relationships with relevant professional bodies are appropriately effective and constructive?

916. How does your organization know that its support services planning and management systems are appropriately effective and constructive?

917. How do you know what, specifically, is required of you in your work?

918. How does your organization know that its system for ensuring a positive organizational climate is appropriately effective and constructive?

919. How does your organization know that its processes for managing severance are appropriately effective, constructive and fair?

3.6 Team Directory: Blue Ocean Strategy

920. Do purchase specifications and configurations match requirements?

921. Process decisions: is work progressing on schedule and per contract requirements?

922. Who will talk to the customer?

923. Who are the Team Members?

924. Have you decided when to celebrate the Blue Ocean Strategy projects completion date?

925. Who will write the meeting minutes and distribute?

926. When will you produce deliverables?

927. Who will be the stakeholders on your next Blue Ocean Strategy project?

928. Why is the work necessary?

929. Days from the time the issue is identified?

930. Contract requirements complied with?

931. Decisions: is the most suitable form of contract being used?

932. When does information need to be distributed?

933. Where should the information be distributed?

934. Decisions: what could be done better to improve the quality of the constructed product?

935. How do unidentified risks impact the outcome of the Blue Ocean Strategy project?

936. What are you going to deliver or accomplish?

937. How and in what format should information be presented?

938. Process decisions: do invoice amounts match accepted work in place?

939. Is construction on schedule?

3.7 Team Operating Agreement: Blue Ocean Strategy

940. Does your team need access to all documents and information at all times?

941. Did you determine the technology methods that best match the messages to be communicated?

942. What resources can be provided for the team in terms of equipment, space, time for training, protected time and space for meetings, and travel allowances?

943. What is teaming?

944. Do you post meeting notes and the recording (if used) and notify participants?

945. What are the current caseload numbers in the unit?

946. Are there more than two functional areas represented by your team?

947. What are some potential sources of conflict among team members?

948. What is your unique contribution to your organization?

949. What types of accommodations will be formulated and put in place for sustaining the team?

950. Do you vary your voice pace, tone and pitch to engage participants and gain involvement?

951. Do you record meetings for the already stated unable to attend?

952. Do you ensure that all participants know how to use the required technology?

953. What is the number of cases currently teamed?

954. Conflict resolution: how will disputes and other conflicts be mediated or resolved?

955. To whom do you deliver your services?

956. What is culture?

957. Have you established procedures that team members can follow to work effectively together, such as a team operating agreement?

958. How will your group handle planned absences?

959. The method to be used in the decision making process; Will it be consensus, majority rule, or the supervisor having the final say?

3.8 Team Performance Assessment: Blue Ocean Strategy

960. To what degree do the goals specify concrete team work products?

961. Do you promptly inform members about major developments that may affect them?

962. What structural changes have you made or are you preparing to make?

963. Can familiarity breed backup?

964. How do you encourage members to learn from each other?

965. To what degree are corresponding categories of skills either actually or potentially represented across the membership?

966. To what degree are the relative importance and priority of the goals clear to all team members?

967. To what degree do members articulate the goals beyond the team membership?

968. Do friends perform better than acquaintances?

969. When does the medium matter?

970. To what degree are sub-teams possible or necessary?

971. What do you think is the most constructive thing that could be done now to resolve considerations and disputes about method variance?

972. To what degree can team members meet frequently enough to accomplish the teams ends?

973. What is method variance?

974. To what degree is the team cognizant of small wins to be celebrated along the way?

975. Can team performance be reliably measured in simulator and live exercises using the same assessment tool?

976. To what degree does the teams work approach provide opportunity for members to engage in fact-based problem solving?

977. If you have received criticism from reviewers that your work suffered from method variance, what was the circumstance?

978. To what degree do all members feel responsible for all agreed-upon measures?

979. To what degree do team members articulate the teams work approach?

3.9 Team Member Performance Assessment: Blue Ocean Strategy

980. How do you determine which data are the most important to use, analyze, or review?

981. What does collaboration look like?

982. What are best practices in use for the performance measurement system?

983. What future plans (e.g., modifications) do you have for your program?

984. What variables that affect team members achievement are within your control?

985. Does the rater (supervisor) have to wait for the interim or final performance assessment review to tell an employee that the employees performance is unsatisfactory?

986. What evaluation results do you have?

987. What changes do you need to make to align practices with beliefs?

988. What are acceptable governance changes?

989. How do you start collaborating?

990. How do you know that all team members are learning?

991. What entity leads the process, selects a potential restructuring option and develops the plan?

992. What is the target group for instruction (e.g., individual and collective or small team instruction)?

993. How do you work together to improve teaching and learning?

994. What makes them effective?

995. To what degree does the teams purpose contain themes that are particularly meaningful and memorable?

996. How are training activities developed from a technical perspective?

997. How should adaptive assessments be implemented?

998. What qualities does a successful Team leader possess?

3.10 Issue Log: Blue Ocean Strategy

999. What is the status of the issue?

1000. In your work, how much time is spent on stakeholder identification?

1001. What is the impact on the risks?

1002. Who do you turn to if you have questions?

1003. Who is the stakeholder?

1004. Are there potential barriers between the team and the stakeholder?

1005. Who is the issue assigned to?

1006. Which team member will work with each stakeholder?

1007. Do you feel more overwhelmed by stakeholders?

1008. Why multiple evaluators?

1009. Who were proponents/opponents?

1010. Are the Blue Ocean Strategy project issues uniquely identified, including to which product they refer?

1011. In classifying stakeholders, which approach to do so are you using?

1012. What is a Stakeholder?

1013. Are there too many who have an interest in some aspect of your work?

1014. Are there common objectives between the team and the stakeholder?

1015. What would have to change?

4.0 Monitoring and Controlling Process Group: Blue Ocean Strategy

1016. Is progress on outcomes due to your program?

1017. How are you doing?

1018. What resources are necessary?

1019. Key stakeholders to work with. How many potential communications channels exist on the Blue Ocean Strategy project?

1020. What areas does the group agree are the biggest success on the Blue Ocean Strategy project?

1021. Do clients benefit (change) from the services?

1022. Is there sufficient time allotted between the general system design and the detailed system design phases?

1023. Feasibility: how much money, time, and effort can you put into this?

1024. How will staff learn how to use the deliverables?

1025. What good practices or successful experiences or transferable examples have been identified?

1026. How many potential communications channels exist on the Blue Ocean Strategy project?

1027. How to ensure validity, quality and consistency?

1028. Overall, how does the program function to serve the clients?

1029. Did the Blue Ocean Strategy project team have the right skills?

1030. Is there sufficient funding available for this?

1031. Is it what was agreed upon?

1032. Did the Blue Ocean Strategy project team have enough people to execute the Blue Ocean Strategy project plan?

4.1 Project Performance Report: Blue Ocean Strategy

1033. To what degree do the structures of the formal organization motivate taskrelevant behavior and facilitate task completion?

1034. To what degree will the approach capitalize on and enhance the skills of all team members in a manner that takes into consideration other demands on members of the team?

1035. To what degree are the goals realistic?

1036. How will procurement be coordinated with other Blue Ocean Strategy project aspects, such as scheduling and performance reporting?

1037. To what degree will the team adopt a concrete, clearly understood, and agreed-upon approach that will result in achievement of the teams goals?

1038. To what degree are the demands of the task compatible with and converge with the mission and functions of the formal organization?

1039. To what degree does the teams approach to its work allow for modification and improvement over time?

1040. To what degree can team members frequently and easily communicate with one another?

1041. To what degree does the funding match the requirement?

1042. To what degree are the tasks requirements reflected in the flow and storage of information?

1043. What is the PRS?

1044. To what degree does the information network provide individuals with the information they require?

1045. What is in it for you?

1046. To what degree does the teams purpose constitute a broader, deeper aspiration than just accomplishing short-term goals?

1047. To what degree are the skill areas critical to team performance present?

1048. To what degree will each member have the opportunity to advance his or her professional skills in all three of the above categories while contributing to the accomplishment of the teams purpose and goals?

1049. To what degree does the formal organization make use of individual resources and meet individual needs?

1050. How is the data used?

4.2 Variance Analysis: Blue Ocean Strategy

1051. Are there changes in the overhead pool and/or organization structures?

1052. Other relevant issues of Variance Analysis -selling price or gross margin?

1053. How have the setting and use of standards changed over time?

1054. Does the contractor use objective results, design reviews and tests to trace schedule performance?

1055. How are material, labor, and overhead variances calculated and recorded?

1056. Why are standard cost systems used?

1057. Historical experience?

1058. Are overhead cost budgets established for each department which has authority to incur overhead costs?

1059. Are all cwbs elements specified for external reporting?

1060. How do you manage changes in the nature of the overhead requirements?

1061. There are detailed schedules which support control account and work package start and completion dates/events?

1062. What are the actual costs to date?

1063. Are significant decision points, constraints, and interfaces identified as key milestones?

1064. Favorable or unfavorable variance?

1065. Are records maintained to show how undistributed budgets are controlled?

1066. Is cost and schedule performance measurement done in a consistent, systematic manner?

4.3 Earned Value Status: Blue Ocean Strategy

1067. Where is evidence-based earned value in your organization reported?

1068. Earned value can be used in almost any Blue Ocean Strategy project situation and in almost any Blue Ocean Strategy project environment. it may be used on large Blue Ocean Strategy projects, medium sized Blue Ocean Strategy projects, tiny Blue Ocean Strategy projects (in cut-down form), complex and simple Blue Ocean Strategy projects and in any market sector. some people, of course, know all about earned value, they have used it for years - but perhaps not as effectively as they could have?

1069. If earned value management (EVM) is so good in determining the true status of a Blue Ocean Strategy project and Blue Ocean Strategy project its completion, why is it that hardly any one uses it in information systems related Blue Ocean Strategy projects?

1070. Are you hitting your Blue Ocean Strategy projects targets?

1071. How much is it going to cost by the finish?

1072. Validation is a process of ensuring that the developed system will actually achieve the stakeholders desired outcomes; Are you building the right product? What do you validate?

1073. How does this compare with other Blue Ocean Strategy projects?

1074. When is it going to finish?

1075. Where are your problem areas?

1076. What is the unit of forecast value?

1077. Verification is a process of ensuring that the developed system satisfies the stakeholders agreements and specifications; Are you building the product right? What do you verify?

4.4 Risk Audit: Blue Ocean Strategy

1078. What impact does prior experience have on decisions made during the risk-assessment process?

1079. Does your organization have a social media policy and procedure?

1080. Do you meet all obligations relating to funds secured from grants, loans and sponsors?

1081. How are risk appetites expressed?

1082. Estimated size of product in number of programs, files, transactions?

1083. Are auditors able to effectively apply more soft evidence found in the risk-assessment process with the results of more tangible audit evidence found through more substantive testing?

1084. What is the effect of globalisation; is business becoming too complex and can the auditor rely on auditing standards?

1085. When your organization is entering into a major contract, does it seek legal advice?

1086. How do you manage risk?

1087. Are Blue Ocean Strategy project requirements stable?

1088. Are audit program plans risk-adjusted?

1089. Do you conduct risk assessments on all programs, activities and events?

1090. Are testing tools available and suitable?

1091. Auditor independence: a burdensome constraint or a core value?

1092. What limitations do auditors face in effectively applying risk-assessment results to the risk of material misstatement measures?

1093. How do you compare to other jurisdictions when managing the risk of ....?

1094. For paid staff, does your organization comply with the minimum conditions for employment and/or the applicable modern award?

1095. Do you have an understanding of insurance claims processes?

1096. Is the auditor able to evaluate contradictory evidence in an unbiased manner?

4.5 Contractor Status Report: Blue Ocean Strategy

1097. What is the average response time for answering a support call?

1098. What was the budget or estimated cost for your organizations services?

1099. What was the overall budget or estimated cost?

1100. What was the actual budget or estimated cost for your organizations services?

1101. How does the proposed individual meet each requirement?

1102. What are the minimum and optimal bandwidth requirements for the proposed soluiton?

1103. Describe how often regular updates are made to the proposed solution. Are corresponding regular updates included in the standard maintenance plan?

1104. Who can list a Blue Ocean Strategy project as organization experience, your organization or a previous employee of your organization?

1105. How long have you been using the services?

1106. If applicable; describe your standard schedule for new software version releases. Are new software version releases included in the standard maintenance plan?

1107. Are there contractual transfer concerns?

1108. How is risk transferred?

1109. What process manages the contracts?

1110. What was the final actual cost?

4.6 Formal Acceptance: Blue Ocean Strategy

1111. Do you perform formal acceptance or burn-in tests?

1112. Does it do what client said it would?

1113. Was the Blue Ocean Strategy project work done on time, within budget, and according to specification?

1114. What can you do better next time?

1115. Was the sponsor/customer satisfied?

1116. What was done right?

1117. What are the requirements against which to test, Who will execute?

1118. Have all comments been addressed?

1119. What lessons were learned about your Blue Ocean Strategy project management methodology?

1120. Is formal acceptance of the Blue Ocean Strategy project product documented and distributed?

1121. Did the Blue Ocean Strategy project manager and team act in a professional and ethical manner?

1122. What is the Acceptance Management Process?

1123. Do you buy-in installation services?

1124. How well did the team follow the methodology?

1125. How does your team plan to obtain formal acceptance on your Blue Ocean Strategy project?

1126. Does it do what Blue Ocean Strategy project team said it would?

1127. General estimate of the costs and times to complete the Blue Ocean Strategy project?

1128. Who supplies data?

1129. Do you buy pre-configured systems or build your own configuration?

1130. What features, practices, and processes proved to be strengths or weaknesses?

5.0 Closing Process Group: Blue Ocean Strategy

1131. What could be done to improve the process?

1132. Is there a clear cause and effect between the activity and the lesson learned?

1133. Were the outcomes different from the already stated planned?

1134. What can you do better next time, and what specific actions can you take to improve?

1135. What was learned?

1136. Did you do what you said you were going to do?

1137. Based on your Blue Ocean Strategy project communication management plan, what worked well?

1138. Is this a follow-on to a previous Blue Ocean Strategy project?

1139. What is the overall risk of the Blue Ocean Strategy project to your organization?

1140. If a risk event occurs, what will you do?

1141. Is the Blue Ocean Strategy project funded?

1142. Were risks identified and mitigated?

1143. What went well?

1144. What is the Blue Ocean Strategy project Management Process?

1145. How will you know you did it?

5.1 Procurement Audit: Blue Ocean Strategy

1146. Is there an approval policy in which the final cost of an order exceeds the amount originally estimated on the requisition or purchase order?

1147. Relevance of the contract to the Internal Market?

1148. Has it been determined which shared services the procurement function/unit should be part of?

1149. Is it calculated whether aggregated procurement can be more cost-efficient?

1150. Does the procurement Blue Ocean Strategy project have a clear goal and does the goal meet the specified needs of the users?

1151. Are the official minutes written in a clear and concise manner?

1152. Was confidentiality ensured when necessary?

1153. Was a formal review of tenders received undertaken?

1154. Was invitation to tender to each specific contract issued after the evaluation of the indicative tenders was completed?

1155. Could bidders learn all relevant information

straight from the tender documents?

1156. Was the payment made to the supplier/contractor within the time frames indicated in the contracts?

1157. Are regulations and protective measures in place to avoid corruption?

1158. Are travel expenditures monitored to determine that they are in line with other employees and reasonable for the area of travel?

1159. Are information technology resources (e-procurement) used to reduce costs?

1160. Are there any complaints of the suppliers and/or end-users?

1161. Where applicable, did your organization adequately manage experts employed to assist in the procurement process?

1162. Does the manual contain policies relating to all business management functions?

1163. Did the chosen procedure ensure competition and transparency?

1164. Who is verifying the performance of the contract and approving payments?

1165. Is an appropriated degree of standardization of goods and services respected?

5.2 Contract Close-Out: Blue Ocean Strategy

1166. Was the contract complete without requiring numerous changes and revisions?

1167. Change in attitude or behavior?

1168. Change in circumstances?

1169. Was the contract type appropriate?

1170. Are the signers the authorized officials?

1171. Change in knowledge?

1172. Have all contracts been completed?

1173. What happens to the recipient of services?

1174. Was the contract sufficiently clear so as not to result in numerous disputes and misunderstandings?

1175. Have all contract records been included in the Blue Ocean Strategy project archives?

1176. Parties: Authorized?

1177. How does it work?

1178. Have all contracts been closed?

1179. What is capture management?

1180. Why Outsource?

1181. How is the contracting office notified of the automatic contract close-out?

1182. Parties: who is involved?

1183. Has each contract been audited to verify acceptance and delivery?

1184. How/when used ?

1185. Have all acceptance criteria been met prior to final payment to contractors?

5.3 Project or Phase Close-Out: Blue Ocean Strategy

1186. What process was planned for managing issues/risks?

1187. In preparing the Lessons Learned report, should it reflect a consensus viewpoint, or should the report reflect the different individual viewpoints?

1188. What was expected from each stakeholder?

1189. How often did each stakeholder need an update?

1190. Can the lesson learned be replicated?

1191. What information is each stakeholder group interested in?

1192. What was the preferred delivery mechanism?

1193. If you were the Blue Ocean Strategy project sponsor, how would you determine which Blue Ocean Strategy project team(s) and/or individuals deserve recognition?

1194. What is this stakeholder expecting?

1195. What information did each stakeholder need to contribute to the Blue Ocean Strategy projects success?

1196. Were cost budgets met?

1197. Was the user/client satisfied with the end product?

1198. What is the information level of detail required for each stakeholder?

1199. Who controlled the resources for the Blue Ocean Strategy project?

1200. What were the actual outcomes?

1201. Did the delivered product meet the specified requirements and goals of the Blue Ocean Strategy project?

1202. When and how were information needs best met?

1203. What benefits or impacts does the stakeholder group expect to obtain as a result of the Blue Ocean Strategy project?

1204. What are the marketing communication needs for each stakeholder?

5.4 Lessons Learned: Blue Ocean Strategy

1205. How effectively were issues managed on the Blue Ocean Strategy project?

1206. Did the Blue Ocean Strategy project improve the team members reputations, skills, personal development?

1207. What solutions or recommendations can you offer that would have improved some aspect of the Blue Ocean Strategy project?

1208. Are there any data that you have overlooked in identifying lessons?

1209. Is the lesson significant, valid, and applicable?

1210. What worked well or did not work well, either for this Blue Ocean Strategy project or for the Blue Ocean Strategy project team?

1211. Were the Blue Ocean Strategy project objectives met (if not, briefly account for what wasnt met)?

1212. How well prepared were you to receive Blue Ocean Strategy project deliverables?

1213. What would you like to see better documented about how to use existing processes on this type of Blue Ocean Strategy project?

1214. How effective were the communications materials in providing and orienting team members about the details of the Blue Ocean Strategy project?

1215. Was there a Blue Ocean Strategy project Definition document. Was there a Blue Ocean Strategy project Plan. Were they used during the Blue Ocean Strategy project?

1216. What on the Blue Ocean Strategy project worked well and was effective in the delivery of the product?

1217. What were the lessons learned on this Blue Ocean Strategy project?

1218. How useful was the format and content of the Blue Ocean Strategy project Status Report to you?

1219. Which estimation issues did you personally have and what was the impact?

1220. Was there enough support – guidance, clerical support, training?

1221. Is your organization willing to expose problems or mistakes for the betterment of the collective whole, and can you do this in a way that does not intimidate employees or workers?

1222. Is there any way in which you think your development process hampered this Blue Ocean Strategy project?

1223. How effective was Blue Ocean Strategy project Team member training?

1224. How much of your time was spent on other than this Blue Ocean Strategy project?

Index

ability   31
absences   234
accept   104, 215
acceptable   50, 145, 237
acceptance   6, 108, 145, 150, 253-254, 260
accepted   184, 232
accepting   196
access 2, 9-10, 59, 143, 197, 233
accomplish   7, 114, 133-134, 194, 232, 236
according   29, 33, 151, 211, 253
account   11, 18, 38, 46, 88, 90, 212, 229, 246, 263
accounted   48
accounting   156, 192
accounts   156
accuracy   50, 54, 150, 186
accurate   10, 110, 146, 193, 200, 214
achievable   117, 194
achieve   7, 68, 75, 83, 100-101, 117, 124, 132, 163, 189-191, 208, 247
achieved   23, 76, 115, 132
acquire   105, 117, 221
acquired   162, 191
across 48, 204, 207, 223, 235
action 42, 47, 78, 86, 90, 132, 142, 190, 202, 214
actionable   229
actioned   178
actions 22, 84, 123, 150, 192, 202, 208, 210, 255
active 139, 142, 152
actively   198
activities   22, 32, 36, 74, 80, 131, 138-139, 143-144, 161, 163, 165, 168, 171, 176, 180, 188, 194, 203, 209, 216, 238, 250
activity 3-4, 37, 161-163, 165-169, 172-174, 176, 180-181, 186, 192, 255
actual 37, 44, 145, 156, 192, 246, 251-252, 262
actually   34, 60, 73, 85, 160, 194, 235, 247
adaptive   238
addition   8, 101
additional   29, 61-62, 64, 66, 159, 182, 193
additions   80
address   21, 71, 134, 196, 222

addressed   85, 169, 218, 229, 253
addressing   31
adequate   35, 141, 159, 213
adequately   29, 52, 61, 157, 229, 258
adherence   97
adjusted   110, 226
adopted   138
adopters   199
adoption   95, 117, 121-122
advance   157, 202, 244
advantage   62, 90, 102, 120
advantages   108, 136, 165
adverse   193
advice 249
affect 59, 89, 131, 142, 148, 151, 153, 172-173, 213, 224, 235, 237
affected   133, 136, 178, 208, 223
affecting   13
afford 203
afterwards   47
against 32, 85, 253
agendas   120
agents 190
aggregate   48
aggregated   257
agreed   46, 54, 159, 242
agreement   5, 113, 119, 233-234
agreements   56, 248
aiming 117
alerts 83
aligned   19
Alignment   142
alleged   1
alliances   114
allies   103
allocate   120, 157
allocated   45, 180
allocating   157, 192
allotted   241
allowances   233
allowed   122, 170-171
allows 10
almost 247

already   156-157, 159, 187, 195, 220, 234, 255
Although   131
altogether   205
always 10
Amazon   11
ambitious   105
amount   152, 257
amounts   232
amplify 59, 109
analysis   3, 6, 12, 42-43, 45-46, 49-50, 53, 58, 61-63, 65, 70, 75, 136, 140, 173, 179, 182, 185, 189, 192, 197, 212-213, 228, 245
analytics   44
analyze   2, 43, 46, 56, 61-62, 76, 206, 237
analyzed   43-44, 52-53, 73, 83, 150, 193, 196, 206
another   11, 108, 155, 163, 172, 243
answer 12-13, 17, 27, 41, 56, 67, 77, 87, 223
answered   26, 40, 55, 66, 76, 86, 129
answering   12, 251
anybody   139
anyone   36, 109
anything   161, 169, 185, 226-227
appeal 94
appealing   45
appear   1, 102
appetites   249
applicable   13, 145, 157, 177, 226, 250-251, 258, 263
applied   83, 192
applying   250
appointed   38-39
approach   48, 68, 104, 108, 113, 214, 221, 236, 239, 243
approaches   69, 75, 98, 198
approval   128, 257
approvals   144, 210
approved   65, 149, 152, 172, 184, 187, 216, 223-225
approving   148, 222, 258
architect   151
Architects   7
archived   173, 179, 184
archives   259
around 119
articulate   235-236
asking 1, 7, 184, 190
aspect 240, 263

aspects   137, 243
aspiration   244
assess 36, 168
assessed   178
assessing   78
Assessment   5, 9-10, 24, 143-144, 195, 202, 204, 235-237
assets 49, 85
assign 25
assigned   32, 39, 133, 154, 157, 176, 178, 192, 239
assigning   170
Assignment   4, 192
assist 9, 68, 84, 172, 180, 183, 200, 226, 258
assistance   39
assistant   7
associated   147, 200, 229
Assume   197, 202-203
Assumption   3, 152
assurance   143, 159, 178, 186, 196-197, 214, 219
assure 54, 61
attached   174
attainable   30, 194
attained   204
attempted   36
attend 234
attendance   39
attendant   76
attended   39
attention   13
attitude   259
attitudes   220
attract 96
attractive   58, 92, 127
attribute   160
attributes   3, 93, 146, 163, 188, 222
audience   94, 107, 112, 123, 125
audiences   112
audited   260
auditing   78, 127, 192, 249
auditor 249-250
auditors   186, 249-250
audits 186
auspices   8
author 1

authority 113, 194-195, 245
authorized 140, 259
automatic 260
available 18-19, 29, 32, 64-65, 84, 141, 162, 167, 176, 186, 197, 200, 205, 209-210, 216-217, 242, 250
Average 13, 26, 40, 55, 66, 76, 86, 129, 175, 226, 251
averse 201
background 11, 121, 165
backup 150, 235
backward 224
balance 42
bandwidth 251
barriers 43, 109, 125, 239
baseline 4, 53, 141, 184
baselined 42, 179
baselines 33, 38
basics 97
become 96, 105, 111, 149, 205, 226
becomes 227
becoming 249
before 10, 36, 151, 162, 167-168, 174, 178
beginning 2, 16, 26, 40, 55, 66, 76, 86, 93, 127, 129
begins 226
behavior 94, 243, 259
behaviors 48, 195, 226
behaviour 228
belief 12, 17, 27, 41, 56, 67, 77, 87, 120
beliefs 237
believable 117
believe 115, 120
benchmark 118, 188
benefit 1, 23, 25, 70, 79, 136, 172, 179, 203, 241
benefits 24, 42, 46-47, 57, 66, 87, 90, 115, 134, 204, 262
best-cost 45
better 7, 31, 53, 96, 110, 161, 183, 226, 232, 235, 253, 255, 263
betterment 264
between 42, 51, 58, 136, 148, 152, 170, 186, 196, 222, 239-241, 255
beyond 235
bidders 145, 257
biggest 50, 67, 241
blinding 60
Blokdyk 8

bodies 229
bottleneck 161
bought 11
bounce 63
boundaries 39
boundary 129
bounds 39
brands 100
Breakdown 3-4, 72, 154-155, 170
briefed 38
briefly 263
brings 39
broader 244
broken 65
budget 72, 83, 162, 174, 176-178, 181, 184, 218, 251, 253
budgeted 44, 158
budgets 125, 156-157, 192-194, 245-246, 262
building 22, 153, 247-248
burden 227
burdensome 250
burn-in 253
business 1, 7, 11, 20, 24, 54, 57-58, 63, 66, 71, 75, 81, 89, 94-96, 99, 102, 105-106, 109, 112-113, 115-117, 121, 126-128, 131-132, 140, 144-147, 157, 206, 210, 218, 224, 249, 258
busywork 131
button 11
buyers 99
buy-in 254
buyout 141
Calculate 123, 166, 173
calculated 158, 245, 257
called 132
campaign 90
cannot 167
canvas 116
capability 46
capable 7, 34
capacities 138
capacity 22, 139
capital 19
capitalize 57, 243
capture 81, 212, 259
captured 47, 74, 142-143, 179, 196, 200

capturing 180
career 148
careers 105
carried 64
cascading 42
caseload 233
categories 235, 244
caused 1
causes 42, 50-51, 56, 60-61, 65, 84, 140, 156, 208
celebrate 231
celebrated 236
center 54
certain 71
chaired 8
challenge 7, 102, 108, 226-227
challenges 27, 32, 102
champion 30
champions 190
chance 208
chances 204
change 5, 17-18, 29, 45, 57, 66-69, 71, 79, 91, 93, 99, 122, 126, 134-135, 140, 144, 150, 155, 160, 167, 190, 200, 202, 207, 213, 215-217, 222-225, 240-241, 259
changed 20, 29, 124-125, 180, 182, 184, 203, 222, 245
changes 22, 35, 38, 43, 47, 52, 62, 64, 69, 76, 80, 87, 102, 104, 108, 122, 128, 140, 146, 151, 156, 170, 172, 184, 187, 204, 222-225, 235, 237, 245, 259
channels 115, 124-125, 216, 241
chargeable 192
charged 42
charges 180
charter 2, 31, 40, 133, 197
charters 36
charts 49, 52, 56
cheaper 53
checked 79-81
checklist 8
checklists 9, 196, 211
choice 52, 110
choose 12, 63, 92, 100, 138
chosen 109, 114, 132, 134, 139, 204, 218-219, 258
circumvent 17
claimed 1

claims 189, 250
clarify 98
classes 196
clearly 12, 17, 20, 27, 32, 36, 41, 56, 58, 67, 77, 87, 107, 194-195, 210-211, 243
clerical 264
client 8, 11, 44, 113, 132, 140, 204, 208, 253, 262
clients 101, 241-242
climate   230
closed 80, 215, 225, 259
closely 11
Close-Out   6, 212, 259-261
Closing 6, 66, 255
Coaches   28, 32, 190
cognizant   236
coherent   214
colleague   121
colleagues   101, 129
collect 59, 86, 128, 182, 190-191
collected   30-31, 42, 45, 58, 61, 64, 73, 150
collection   42, 49, 51, 53, 65, 191
collective   238, 264
colour 111
combine   75
coming   64, 212
command   204
comments   213, 253
commercial   157
commitment   98, 123, 139
committed   27, 60, 152, 178, 200, 214
committee   142-143, 152
common   134, 180, 197, 240
community   22, 102, 117, 145, 174, 182, 208
communitys   110
companies   1, 8, 85, 106, 110, 117, 172-173, 226
company   7, 53, 105, 109, 121
compare   59, 68, 203, 248, 250
compared   94, 156
comparing   69, 156
comparison   12, 193, 212-213
compatible   224, 243
compelling   29
compete   94

competency 107
competing 104, 116
competitor 90
compilers 200
complaint 228
complaints 189, 228, 258
complete 1, 9, 12, 37, 46, 141, 150, 159, 161, 163, 167, 170, 174, 189, 197, 200, 204, 214, 254, 259
completed 13, 28, 30, 35-36, 55, 143, 150-151, 167-168, 178, 257, 259
completely 174, 205
completing 102, 154
completion 36-37, 132, 156, 167, 192, 231, 243, 246-247
complex 7, 45, 96, 141, 176, 247, 249
complexity 48, 62, 150, 196
compliance 51-52, 64
complied 231
comply 250
components 49, 52, 152, 186, 214
comprise 138
compute 13
concept 99, 166
Concern 50, 194
concerned 21
concerns 21, 43, 252
concise 257
concisely 107
conclusion 49
concrete 235, 243
condition 78, 176
conditions 81, 108, 250
conduct 186, 250
conducted 73, 111, 143, 185, 189, 210, 212
confirm 13
Conflict 233-234
conflicts 176, 234
conform 153
conjure 146
consensus 234, 261
consider 17-18, 22, 99, 172, 212
considered 19, 23, 42, 115-116, 119, 214, 227
consist 157
consistent 38, 43, 56, 78, 103, 111, 157-158, 246

consortium	204
constantly	198
constitute	244
Constraint	3, 152, 250
consultant	7, 142, 181
consulted	120, 193
consulting	51
consumer	91, 94, 103, 106, 124, 129
consumers	103, 125
contact	7, 214
contacts	118
contain	19, 56, 80, 238, 258
contained	1
contains	9
content	30, 140, 229, 264
contents	1-2, 9
context	23, 28, 35, 37, 172
continual	11, 80, 84
continuing	229
contract	6, 156, 180, 192, 211, 221, 231, 249, 257-260
contractor	6, 178, 180, 192, 245, 251, 258
contracts	56, 157, 179, 210, 252, 258-259
contribute	261
control	2, 65, 72, 77, 79-82, 85, 132, 150, 156, 182, 204, 210, 214, 222-223, 227, 237, 246
controlled	246, 262
controls	19, 57, 64, 71, 74, 79, 83, 142, 202
convention	94
converge	243
convey	1
cooperate	183
copying	110
Copyright	1
correct	41, 77, 177
corrected	178
correction	156
corrective	84, 210
correctly	138
correspond	9, 11
corruption	258
counsel	74
counting	94, 162
country	99

counts 94
course 29, 45, 109, 247
covering   9, 83
co-workers   125
create 11, 23, 95-96, 108-109, 127, 145, 222
created   59, 61, 88-89, 102, 119-120, 135, 138, 140, 196, 208, 211
creating   7, 50, 88, 150
creative   74
creativity   68
credible   183
crisis   22
criteria 2, 5, 9, 11, 30, 58, 68, 78, 90, 130, 132, 142, 145, 148, 160, 182, 210, 212-213, 260
CRITERION   2, 17, 27, 41, 56, 67, 77, 87
critical 30-31, 35, 59, 72, 78, 83, 85, 160-161, 165, 219, 226-227, 244
criticism   61, 236
crucial 62, 218
crystal 13
cultural 71
culture 126, 194-195, 234
current 35, 41, 47, 51, 57-59, 69, 88, 93, 105, 116, 118, 120, 159, 172, 187, 191, 202, 216, 233
currently   29, 121, 234
custom 18
customer   11, 17, 21-22, 30-33, 35, 45, 75, 80, 84, 89, 97-98, 101, 108, 111, 115-117, 121, 123, 125, 127, 134, 146-147, 150, 180, 184, 187, 205-206, 231, 253
customers   1, 25, 28, 31, 38, 44, 46, 57, 59, 73, 89, 92-93, 96, 103-105, 107, 111, 113, 115, 122, 124-125, 128-129, 137, 147, 197, 209, 221
cut-down   247
cutting 204, 207
cycles 88, 134
damage   1, 204
Dashboard   9
dashboards   80
databases   191
day-to-day   84, 165
deadlines   19, 92
dealing   18, 121
decide 72-73, 195

decided 231
deciding 121
decision 5, 54, 57, 66, 68, 72-74, 197, 226-227, 234, 246
decisions 68-69, 71-72, 74, 82, 85, 195-196, 218, 227, 231-232, 249
dedicated 7
deeper 13, 244
defect 46, 196
defective 200
defects 47
define 2, 23, 27-28, 33-34, 43, 61, 67, 134, 146, 154, 172, 174, 188, 227
defined 12-13, 17, 19, 27-28, 32-34, 36-38, 41, 47, 56, 63, 67, 77, 87, 142, 154, 157, 159-160, 173, 176, 178, 184, 186, 188, 194-195, 197, 210-211, 218
defines 33
defining 7, 210
definite 80
definition 20, 33, 143, 173, 191, 264
degree 91, 235-236, 238, 243-244, 258
delayed 166
delaying 47
delays 52, 161, 174
delegated 34
deletions 80
deliver 25, 35, 75, 115, 119, 123, 183, 232, 234
delivered 53, 90, 101, 107, 160, 171, 215, 262
delivers 170
delivery 24, 88, 108, 139, 200, 207, 260-261, 264
demand 103, 205
demands 243
department 7, 109, 220, 245
depend 221
dependent 88, 144
deploy 78, 92, 128
deployed 79
deploying 51
deployment 48
derive 78
Describe 73, 125, 148, 166, 215, 251
described 1, 147, 157, 184, 225
describing 28
deserve 261

deserving 220
design 1, 8, 11, 71, 73, 126, 152, 214-215, 241, 245
designated 160
designed 7, 11, 62, 70, 75
designing 7
desired 29, 63, 170, 224, 247
detail 48, 75, 134, 154, 163, 174, 229, 262
detailed 57, 59, 145, 157, 160, 162, 179, 196, 241, 246
details 217, 264
detect 81
determine 11-12, 92-93, 162, 173, 182, 197, 211, 213, 233, 237, 258, 261
determined 60, 190, 257
determines 53, 180
develop 54, 67-69, 72, 144, 154-155, 202-203, 215
developed 8, 11, 30, 33, 36, 40, 52, 68, 71, 143, 159, 166, 185, 187, 191, 196-197, 210, 216-217, 224, 238, 247-248
developers 201
developing 60, 70, 73, 138
develops 238
device 229
devices 229
diagnostic 208
diagram 3, 61, 124, 167-168
Dictionary 3, 156
differ 111, 219
difference 138, 170, 186, 226
different 7, 21, 28, 33-34, 38, 61, 93, 101, 113, 159, 172, 226, 255, 261
difficult 61, 107, 143, 161, 163, 165, 171, 184
difficulty 204
digital 85
direct 156-157, 192
direction 29, 53, 140
directions 208
directly 1, 57, 59, 131, 198
Directory 5, 231
Disagree 12, 17, 27, 41, 56, 67, 77, 87
disaster 48
disastrous 54
disclosure 85
discovered 76
discrete 157

discussion 42
display 52
displayed 31, 42, 49, 52, 64, 161
disposal 18, 229
dispose 111
disposed 184
disputes 234, 236, 259
disqualify 60
disrupt 126
disruptive 57
distribute 215, 231
diversify 90
Divided 26, 34, 40, 55, 66, 76, 86, 129
division 141
document 11, 35, 151-152, 226, 264
documented 33, 52, 78-79, 84, 146, 150, 159, 173, 184, 194, 196, 211, 213, 218, 228, 253, 263
documents 7, 151, 172-173, 179, 188, 233, 258
dollars 192
dominant 108
dormant 118
dramatic 103
drives 51
driving 113, 120, 122
Duration 4, 139, 155, 172-174
durations 37, 159, 177
during 29, 70, 164, 169, 196, 200, 205, 209, 212, 229, 249, 264
duties 222
dynamic 48, 110
dynamics 35
earlier 122
earned 6, 157, 180, 247
earning 173
easily 243
economic 108, 208
economy 172
ecosystem 101
eDiscovery 226
edition 9
editorial 1
educate 111
education 24, 84, 229
effect 52, 202, 204, 207, 249, 255

effective 21-22, 106, 112, 146, 174, 186, 188, 208, 213, 226, 228-230, 238, 264
effects 46, 165-166, 198
efficiency 82
efficient 125, 138, 179, 221
effort 39, 45, 47, 51, 91, 101, 152, 156, 214, 241
efforts 36, 76, 133, 178
either 235, 263
electronic 1
elements 11-12, 102-103, 113, 157, 214, 218, 245
Elevator 147
elicit 190
eliminate 208
eliminated 94, 193
embarking 29
emergent 48
emerging 63, 80
emotion 93
emotional 94
employ 114
employed 258
employee 73, 116, 237, 251
employees 20, 63, 115, 129, 228, 237, 258, 264
employers 135
employment 250
empower 7
empowered 188
enable 57
enablers 37, 98, 106
encourage 68, 81, 124, 126, 235
end-users 200, 258
engage 101, 124, 234, 236
engagement 135, 198, 202
enhance 77, 111, 243
enhanced 105
enhancing 80
enough 7, 49, 65, 108, 146, 148, 236, 242, 264
ensure 32, 37, 76, 92, 97, 108, 114, 124, 139, 142, 145, 152, 186, 190, 234, 242, 258
ensured 257
ensures 92
ensuring 10, 138, 230, 247-248
entail 51

entering 249
Enterprise 220
entire 156, 204, 207
entities 42
entity 1, 238
entrants 23
envisaged 139
equipment 22, 24, 131, 233
equipped 32
equitably 34
errors 123, 156, 180
essential 115
establish 67, 78, 182
estimate 42, 50, 141, 216, 254
estimated 36-37, 42-43, 182-183, 212, 249, 251, 257
estimates 4, 39, 48, 60, 138, 156, 172, 178, 180, 185, 196, 210
estimating 4, 160, 174, 179, 182-183
estimation 138, 264
ethical 115, 253
ethics 106, 206
ethnic 109
evaluate 71, 137, 142, 250
evaluating 68
evaluation 58, 188, 212-213, 237, 257
evaluators 212, 239
events 42, 74, 133, 173, 246, 250
everyday 63
everyone 32, 34, 228
everything 226
evidence 13, 202, 221, 249-250
evolution 41
evolve 82
evolving 101
exactly 188
example 2, 9, 14, 24, 59, 81, 140
examples 7, 9, 11, 241
exceed 155
exceeds 257
excellence 7
excellent 50
except 156
excess 115, 156

exclude 69
execute 113, 242, 253
executed 42, 49, 225
Executing 5, 218
execution 20, 78
executions 74
executive 7, 117
exercises 236
existence 206
existing 11-12, 81, 91, 133, 144, 151, 263
exists 92, 102
expand 112, 129
expect 108, 262
expected 24, 37, 104, 124, 131-132, 140, 173, 181, 226, 261
expecting 261
expend 51
expensive 45
experience 100, 121, 165, 194, 204, 245, 249, 251
expert 39
expertise 75
experts 30, 258
explained 11
explicit 191
exploit 95
explore 61
explored 206
expose 264
express 137
expressed 249
extent 12, 21, 23, 29, 139, 156, 204
external 36, 104, 143, 157, 188, 199, 205, 245
extreme 49
facilitate 12, 24, 80, 243
facilities 147
facing 17
fact-based 236
factors 28, 43, 47, 68, 79, 82, 86, 88-89, 98, 102, 116, 119, 122, 167, 183, 218
failure 53, 95, 188
fairly 33
familiar 9, 59, 112
fashion 1, 39
fashions 101

Favorable	246
feasible	50, 126, 182, 202
feature	10
features	106, 112, 254
feedback	2, 11, 30, 32, 128
figure	46
finalize	212
finalized	14
financial	57, 60, 64, 87, 89, 119, 200, 203, 228
finding	101
findings	188
fingertips	10
finish	133, 161-162, 247-248
finished	165
flexible	54
focused	48, 54, 197
follow	11, 79, 119, 125, 139, 167, 215, 219, 234, 254
followed	35, 178, 200, 211
follower	105
following	9, 12, 107
follow-on	255
follow-up	139
for--and	85
forces	81, 106, 122
forecast	248
forefront	120
foreign	89
forever	125
forget	10
formal	6, 96, 153, 197, 206, 243-244, 253-254, 257
formally	152, 196, 215
format	11, 232, 264
formats	203
formed	27, 32
forming	152
formula	13
Formulate	27
formulated	140, 233
forward	97, 113
foster	93, 202
founder	95
Fragmented	104
frames	258

framework 190
frequency 78, 127
frequent 160
frequently 46, 236, 243
friend 121
friends 235
frontiers 68
full-scale 71
fulltime 178, 214
function 159, 242, 257
functional 156, 192, 233
functions 91, 106, 109, 112, 123, 146-147, 171, 178, 194, 243, 258
funded 255
funding 108-109, 144, 242, 244
further 193, 202
future 7, 45, 52, 79, 106, 110, 204-205, 237
gained 61, 82, 84
gather 12, 28-29, 34, 40-41, 57, 60
gathered 44, 59-60, 62-64
gathering 34, 146, 173, 215
general 133, 163, 241, 254
generally 221
generate 60, 62, 70
generated 57, 73
generation 9, 64
generators 200
Gerardus 8
getting 88, 226
Global 106, 165
governance 22, 91, 196, 237
governing 228
Government 157
graded 203
granted 94
grants 249
graphics 21
graphs 9, 49
greater 140
greatest 122
ground 41, 57
grouped 163
groups 98, 137, 152, 171, 178, 193, 221

growth 60, 98
guarantee 74
guaranteed 31
guidance 1, 188, 264
guidelines 226
hampered 264
handle 169, 206, 209, 234
handled 213
handling 204, 228
happen 19, 122, 203, 208-209, 223
happened 223
happening 57
happens 7, 11, 35, 46, 108, 116, 120, 124, 182, 202-203, 208, 228, 259
hardest 42
hardly 247
havent 88
having 202, 234
hazards 208-209
health 100, 117, 214
healthy 229
hearing 109
helpful 44
helping 7, 134
highest 20
high-level 35-36, 133
highlight 202
highly 115
hijacking 116
hinder 109
hiring 80
Historical 182, 245
history 161, 184
hitters 56
hitting 247
hoping 134
horizontal 136
humans 7
hurdles 95, 117, 121
hypotheses 56
identified 1, 23, 25, 31, 33, 35, 43, 47-48, 53-54, 58, 61, 66, 70, 131, 138, 142, 153, 156, 159-160, 173, 178, 184, 188, 193-194, 196, 200, 205, 210, 212, 214, 226, 231, 239, 241, 246, 255

identify 12, 25, 43, 46, 59, 63, 133, 182, 192, 229
identities 96
images 146
imbalance 103
imbedded 82
immediate 41
impact 5, 29, 31, 46-50, 52-55, 72, 138, 144, 184-185, 202-204, 206, 213, 216, 225, 232, 239, 249, 264
impacted 151
impacts 175, 262
imperative 106
implement 21-22, 51, 77, 97
importance 235
important 20, 22-23, 38, 43, 54, 57, 59, 106, 109, 115-116, 118, 189, 198, 237
improve 2, 11-12, 63, 67-68, 70-71, 73-76, 132, 181, 187, 192, 210, 232, 238, 255, 263
improved 70-71, 74-75, 86, 213, 263
improving 220
inaccurate 145
incentives 80, 95, 97, 102, 104, 124
include 24, 69, 75, 156, 213
included 2, 9, 146-147, 174, 180, 183, 222, 251, 259
includes 10, 49
including 28, 31-32, 51, 72, 86, 133, 156, 228, 239
inclusion 228
incomplete 145
increased 102
increasing 105
incurred 45
in-depth 9, 12
indicate 48, 60, 78, 90
indicated 84, 258
indicating 91
indicative 257
indicators 23, 43, 57, 59, 65, 69, 205
indirect 42, 156-157, 180, 192-193
indirectly 1
individual 1, 55, 131, 138, 161, 176, 238, 244, 251, 261
industries 111, 125
industry 19, 23, 28-29, 52, 58, 89, 92, 94-96, 98-99, 101-102, 104, 113, 119-120, 122, 125, 127, 197
industrys 79, 82-83, 86, 108

influence   68, 100, 113, 135, 194, 199
influences   91, 104, 137, 165, 199
influx   89
inform 235
informed   125, 193
ingrained   85
inhibit 71
initial   34, 121, 134
initially 145
initiated   151, 182, 224
initiating   2, 108, 131, 152
initiative   12, 190, 216
innovate   67, 126
innovation   24, 33, 66, 91, 93, 95, 97, 100, 102, 104-105, 109, 114, 124, 126, 128
innovative   108, 137, 183
in-process   65
inputs   28, 38, 44, 64, 81, 142
insight 62, 65
insights 9
install 107
Instead 118
insurance   250
insure   97
integrate   86, 126, 139
integrated   205
integrity   20, 117, 225
intended   1, 68-69
INTENT 17, 27, 41, 56, 67, 77, 87
intention   1
intents 138
interact   123
interest 112, 209, 221, 240
interested   127, 261
interests   46
interfaces   246
interim 92, 237
internal   1, 36, 104, 122, 136, 152, 160, 188, 199, 257
internally   103
interpret   12-13
intervals   160
interview   93
intimidate   264

introduce   48, 201
introduced   151
invaluable   2, 11
inventory   156
invest   115
investment   21, 63, 91, 191, 206
investor   42
invitation   257
invoice 232
invoke   93
involve 118, 136
involved   23, 25, 36, 52, 70, 137, 152, 160, 173, 179, 218-219, 221, 260
involves   78, 91
isolate   50
issued   23, 188, 257
issues   18, 20, 22-23, 25, 76, 150-151, 153, 169, 176, 178, 197, 214, 228, 239, 245, 261, 263-264
iteration   178
Iterative   139
itself   1, 21, 159
judgment   1
justified 132, 152
killer   108
kinked   103
knowledge   11, 36-37, 61, 75, 77, 79-80, 82, 84, 92-93, 194, 217, 259
larger   54
largest 173
latest   9, 156
leader 22, 30, 69, 89, 94, 107, 204, 238
leaders 32, 63, 92, 94, 123, 199
leadership   33-34, 92, 100, 139
league 94
learned   6, 81, 253, 255, 261, 263-264
learning   77, 79, 226, 237-238
legally   229
legend 120
lesson   255, 261, 263
lessons 6, 71, 81, 253, 261, 263-264
levels   20, 57, 59, 69, 79, 100, 155-156, 187
leverage   28, 81, 91, 123, 182, 216
leveraged   36

liability 1
licensed 1
lifecycle 45, 112
life-cycle 50
lifecycles 75
Lifetime 10
likelihood 68, 76, 202
likely 121, 173, 203-205, 212, 226-227
limitation 41
limited 11, 194
limits 104
linked 33, 104, 227
liquidity 115
listed 1
litter 44
loaded 213
locally 160
located 160
logged 222
logical 168-169
long-term 85, 90, 114
looking 127, 181
losses 52
lowest 167
luxury 129
maintain 77, 117, 122
maintained 156, 229, 246
majority 234
makers 54, 85, 197
making 22, 66, 68-69, 72, 190, 234
manage 28, 38, 55, 75, 131, 141-142, 148, 150, 153, 165, 176, 185-186, 193, 206, 245, 249, 258
manageable 29, 214
managed 7, 38, 79, 142, 151, 222, 263
management 1, 3-5, 9, 11-12, 21-22, 28, 31-32, 72, 95, 101, 109, 112, 136, 140, 142, 144, 151-152, 159-160, 170, 172-173, 178, 180-181, 184-186, 188, 192-193, 195-198, 200, 203, 205, 210, 213-214, 216, 218, 220-221, 227, 229, 247, 253, 255-256, 258-259
manager 7, 12, 18, 32, 37, 92, 131, 134, 142, 160, 186, 212, 220, 253
managers 2, 72, 130, 172
manages 252
managing 2, 73, 130, 135, 207, 228, 230, 250, 261

Mandated 207
mandatory 224
manner 157-158, 179, 186, 192, 218, 222, 243, 246, 250, 253, 257
mantle 105
manual 258
mapped 28
mapping 96, 219
margin 245
marked 150
market 22, 44, 96, 101, 107, 114-115, 121, 123-125, 129, 133, 172, 247, 257
marketer 7
marketing 104, 120, 125, 262
markets 22, 122, 136
material 133, 156-157, 189, 245, 250
materials 1, 179, 216, 264
matrices 148
Matrix 3-5, 136, 148, 192-193, 206
matter 30, 43, 98, 235
matters 226
maturing 204
maximize 88
maximizing 172
meaningful 238
measurable 30, 133, 180
measure 2, 12, 20, 28, 37, 41-43, 45-47, 50, 52-53, 55, 64, 67, 69, 73, 80-82, 85, 133, 136, 139, 159, 182
measured 21, 42, 46, 53, 81, 186, 188, 236
measures 42-44, 48, 54-55, 57, 59, 61, 65, 69, 78, 138, 187, 191, 208, 236, 250, 258
measuring 80
mechanical 1
mechanism 207, 261
mechanisms 136, 139
mediated 234
medium 235, 247
meeting 30, 80, 191, 198, 221, 226, 231, 233
meetings 31, 38-39, 145, 160, 197, 226, 233-234
megatrends 99
member 5, 33, 100, 127, 220, 237, 239, 244, 264
members 28, 31, 34-35, 39, 63, 84, 150, 160, 173, 178-179, 198, 204, 211, 214, 231, 233-237, 243, 263-264

membership 235
memorable 238
mentors 200
message 24, 216-217
messages 198, 233
method 53, 138, 174, 179, 198, 234, 236
methods 32, 50, 60, 178, 182, 206, 216, 228, 233
metrics 4, 37, 46-47, 63, 80, 82, 115, 134, 142, 180, 185, 188-189, 196-197, 206
milestone 3, 133, 165, 210
milestones 31, 135, 168, 246
minimise 217
Minimize 138, 200
minimum 126, 229, 250-251
minutes 30, 72, 231, 257
missed 109
missing 163, 184
mission 98, 107, 111, 133, 195, 243
mistakes 264
mitigate 150
mitigated 255
mitigating 196
mitigation 140, 177, 201, 214
mix-ups 229
Modeling 191
models 22, 65, 106, 153
modern 250
modified 70, 78
module 144
moments 62
momentum 109
monitor 69, 79, 82, 85, 136, 142, 159, 182, 204
monitored 82-83, 162, 174, 197, 258
monitoring 6, 80, 84, 169, 204-205, 241
months 67, 72
motivate 89, 112, 243
motivation 20, 78
motive 190
moving 97
multiple 239
narrow 65
national 208
nature 48, 245

nearest 13
necessary 58, 65, 68, 104, 108, 128, 138, 182, 200, 210, 224, 231, 235, 241, 257
needed 17, 19, 22, 24, 38, 64, 77, 83, 174, 197, 219
negative 55, 216-217
negotiated 113
neither 1
network 3, 167-168, 244
Neutral 12, 17, 27, 41, 56, 67, 77, 87
non-Blue 144
normal 85, 129
normalized 212
notice 1, 139
noticing 227
notified 260
notify 233
number 26, 40, 55, 66, 76, 86, 129, 163, 171, 173, 234, 249, 266
numbers 233
numerous 259
objective 7, 54-55, 133, 180, 227, 245
objectives 19, 22-23, 27, 33, 37, 78, 86, 90, 107-108, 116, 119, 142, 176, 179, 197, 208, 221, 240, 263
observe 195
observed 71
obsolete 99
obstacles 17, 91, 104, 122, 183
obtain 173, 254, 262
obtained 30, 43, 210
obtaining 44
obviously 13
occasions 124
occupy 114
occurring 69
occurs 22, 48, 131, 188, 206, 255
oceans 103
offered 89, 102, 119
offerings 59, 68
offers 212
office 212, 220, 260
officers 212
official 257
officials 259

one-time   7
ongoing   45, 81, 162, 174
on-going   142, 159
online 11, 91
operate   208
operates   121
operating   5, 43, 78, 129, 138, 233-234
operation   80, 174
operations   12, 80, 85-86
operators   79
opponent   226-227
opponents   103, 239
opposed   198
opposite   120-121
opposition   105
optimal   70, 251
optimize   68, 80
optimiztic   173
option 238
options 18, 172
organize   79
organized   163
orient 80
oriented   196
orienting   264
original 177, 227
originally   159, 257
originate   85
others 172, 182-183, 189, 193, 226
otherwise   1, 71, 184
outcome   13, 74, 134, 170, 232
outcomes   43, 70, 74, 80, 101, 118, 136, 183, 241, 247, 255, 262
outlined   78
outlook   58
output 28, 54, 58, 61-63, 65, 78, 81
outputs   28, 56, 63-65, 81, 169, 173, 215
outside 68, 99, 131, 133, 197, 219
Outsource   260
outweigh   42, 204
overall 12-13, 19, 86, 89, 100, 168, 204, 242, 251, 255
overcome   32, 104, 183
overhead   156-157, 192, 245

overheads 143, 196
overlooked 263
oversight 142, 152
overtime 164
owners 154
ownership 36, 84
package 192, 246
packages 157
paradigm 95
paradigms 105
paragraph 129
parallel 167
parameters 78
Pareto 56
particular 44, 59
Parties 259-260
partners 25, 36, 92, 110, 115, 118, 138
pattern 163
payment 258, 260
payments 211, 258
pending 225
people 7, 25, 50, 61, 69-70, 81, 85, 89, 100, 105, 108, 118, 120, 123-124, 136, 172-173, 190, 193, 208, 220, 242, 247
percent 122
percentage 148
perform 25, 31, 34, 39, 141, 144, 171, 186, 209, 222, 235, 253
performed 50, 148, 158, 180
performing 157
perhaps 20, 247
period 157, 203
permission 1
permit 48
person 1
personal 263
personally 148, 264
personnel 83, 167, 190, 196, 229
pertaining 131
pertinent 83
phases 45, 138, 145, 198, 241
pioneer 120
places 180
planet 85

planned   42, 49, 78, 145, 156-158, 161, 175, 202, 234, 255, 261
planners   85
planning   3, 9, 84, 131, 138-139, 142, 151, 167, 169-170, 187, 192, 220, 228-229
players 99, 101
please 212
pocket 175
pockets   175
points 25, 40, 55, 66, 76, 86, 129, 166, 191, 246
policies   142, 195, 216, 258
policy 37, 85, 136, 169, 196, 249, 257
political   71, 109, 138, 199, 206
population   139
portray 56
position   105, 116
positioned   98-99, 183
positions   114
positive   67, 109, 140, 198, 230
possess 238
possible   47, 60, 65, 70, 73, 77, 126, 174, 196, 204, 235
potential   23, 43, 47, 60, 68-69, 71, 97, 99, 114, 157, 173, 203-204, 214, 233, 238-239, 241
practical   67, 73, 77, 220-221
practice   136, 205
practices   1, 11, 80-81, 237, 241, 254
precaution   1
precede   172
predicting   80
predictor   171
preference   124
preferred   261
pre-filled   9
prepare   172, 190, 198
prepared   121, 263
preparing   235, 261
present   45, 79, 110, 122, 206, 244
presented   21, 232
preserve   39, 98
prevail 90
prevent   52, 153, 213
prevented   229
preventive   208

prevents 22
previous 36, 165, 177, 251, 255
previously 224
priced 113
prices 212
pricing 111, 116
primarily 197
primary 49, 145, 171
printing 8
priorities 44, 48
priority 44, 48, 235
privacy 188
private 91
probably 170
problem 17-18, 20-21, 23-24, 27, 29-31, 36, 49, 60, 220, 236, 248
problems 17, 19, 50, 68-69, 84, 138, 150, 264
procedure 229, 249, 258
procedures 11, 78-79, 84, 152-153, 169, 184, 187, 190, 197, 210, 216, 234
proceeding 174
process 1-7, 11, 28, 33-36, 38, 42, 46-49, 52, 54, 57-59, 61-65, 69-71, 78-81, 83-86, 131, 138, 142, 144, 148, 150-153, 159, 169, 173-174, 178, 181, 187, 190-191, 200-201, 205-206, 215, 218, 227, 231-232, 234, 238, 241, 247-249, 252-253, 255-256, 258, 261, 264
processes 28, 52, 57-58, 62, 65-66, 80-81, 132, 139, 152, 160, 191-192, 203, 211, 218-219, 224, 230, 250, 254, 263
procuring 142
produce 132, 169, 221, 231
produced 62, 67
producing 148
product 1, 11, 18-20, 23, 28, 36, 39, 42, 57, 59, 83, 88, 93, 95, 101, 104, 107-108, 111-112, 119-120, 122, 126-127, 133, 151, 166, 184, 187, 200, 209, 219-221, 224, 232, 239, 247-249, 253, 262, 264
products 1, 19, 21, 24, 50, 73, 92, 101, 104, 111-112, 116, 133, 138-139, 145, 148, 218, 221, 224, 235
profile 228
profit 108, 127
profitable 120, 124
program 22, 42, 133, 138-139, 181, 237, 241-242, 249
programs 97, 220, 228, 249-250
progress 38, 86, 133, 139, 182, 190, 218, 241

prohibited 156
project 2-4, 6-7, 9, 18, 25, 30, 78-79, 82, 88, 92, 96, 109, 118, 130-145, 148, 150-155, 159-163, 165, 167-168, 170-184, 186-187, 193-198, 200, 202-205, 207, 210, 212, 214-215, 218-220, 224-225, 231-232, 239, 241-243, 247, 249, 251, 253-257, 259, 261-265
projected 157
projection 204
projects 2, 88, 97, 110, 122, 130, 148, 150-151, 153-154, 172, 176, 195, 206, 220-221, 231, 247-248, 261
promising 108
promote 50, 61
promptly 235
proofing 71
proper 85, 144
properly 11, 32, 52
property 228
proponents 239
proposal 165, 213
proposals 85, 173, 212-213
proposed 22, 43, 70, 74, 136, 145, 203, 214, 251
protect 57, 117
protected 233
protective 258
protocols 97, 189
proved 254
provide 22, 65, 117, 128, 135, 141, 147, 156-157, 173, 183, 188, 192, 236, 244
provided 8, 13, 83, 159-160, 178, 213, 233
provider 45, 216
provides 146, 170, 229
providing 85, 135, 176, 264
provision 178
published 179, 216
publisher 1
pulled 122
purchase 9, 11, 124, 212, 231, 257
purchased 11, 156
purchases 214
purpose 2, 11, 98, 133, 170-171, 183, 190, 222, 226, 238, 244
pursuing 91
qualified 34, 61, 63-64, 141
qualifies 59

qualify 61-62
qualities   34, 238
quality 1, 4-5, 11, 43-44, 51, 58, 62, 77, 97-99, 132, 139, 142-143, 159, 178, 185-186, 188, 190-191, 194-197, 210-211, 213-214, 219, 228, 232, 242
quantified   49
question   12-13, 17, 27, 41, 56, 67, 77, 87, 116, 138, 190
questions   7, 9, 12, 199, 239
quickly 12, 59, 63
radical 128
radically   57
raised 82-83, 88, 150, 178
ranking 222
rather 48, 125
ratings 213
rational   157, 192
reached   20, 125
reaching   125
reaction   90, 204
reactivate   118
readiness   143
readings   79
realism 212
realistic   20, 95, 177, 243
realize 45, 87
really 7, 38, 88, 92, 101, 193
reason 120, 216
reasonable   160, 178, 180, 210, 258
reasons   29, 114, 189
reassess   178
re-assign   163
rebuild 108
recast 181
receipt 229
receive   9-10, 37, 44, 198, 212, 263
received   38, 213-214, 228, 236, 257
recently   11, 117
recession   126
recipient   23, 259
recognize   2, 17, 19, 21-22, 54
recognized   18, 20, 23, 64, 199
recognizes   18
recommend   121, 150

recommends 104
record 190, 234
recorded 187, 222, 245
recording 1, 233
records 64, 126, 156, 186, 192, 229, 246, 259
recovery 177
recruiting 172
redefine 20
re-design 65
reduce 44, 47, 75, 152, 159, 192, 202, 227, 258
reduced 79, 86, 113, 208
reducing 80, 105
references 266
reflect 61, 123, 214, 261
reflected 244
reform 85, 118
reforms 22, 50
refuses 208
regard 85
regarding 120, 220
Register 2, 4, 135, 202-203
regular 38-39, 65, 251
regularly 31, 35, 39, 116, 197
regulatory 214
reinforce 98, 110
reinforced 138
rejected 222
relate 57, 90, 218, 224
related 22, 51, 58, 82, 150, 156, 187, 198, 247
relating 249, 258
relation 22, 98, 137
relations 202
relative 86, 235
relatively 96
release 82, 178-179, 198
releases 251
Relevance 257
relevant 11, 30, 42, 65, 160, 229, 245, 257
reliable 32, 97, 208
reliably 236
relocation 141
remain 33
remaining 89, 177, 182

remedial 52
remedies 41
remember 174
remove 76, 208
remunerate 72
repair 196, 229
repeat 139
rephrased 11
replace 133
replacing 144
replicated 261
Report 5-6, 73, 79, 220, 228, 243, 251, 261, 264
reported 157, 188, 210, 247
reporting 83, 100, 144, 157, 203, 243, 245
reports 44, 135, 160, 180, 214
repository 143, 179, 197
represent 224
reproduced 1
reputation 119
request 5, 222-225
requested 1, 69, 212, 222, 224
requests 212, 222-223
require 36, 39, 78, 81, 133, 169, 176, 202, 244
required 24, 37-38, 76, 132, 146-147, 161-163, 167, 174, 181, 191, 194, 216, 229, 234, 262
requires 131
requiring 135, 259
research 22, 108, 121, 172
reserved 1
reserves 196
reside 181, 197
residual 156
resolution 65, 234
resolve 163, 236
resolved 179, 234
resource 3-4, 88, 110, 145, 163, 169-172, 196, 220
resources 2, 9, 19, 21, 29, 32, 35, 42, 63, 72, 76, 83, 88-89, 95, 120, 131-133, 142, 159, 162-163, 167, 170, 182, 193, 219, 233, 241, 244, 258, 262
respect 1
respected 57, 258
respond 138, 202, 216
responded 13

response   22, 78-80, 82, 84, 213, 216, 251
responses   202, 213
responsive   174, 182
restrict 146
result   66-67, 151, 181-182, 184, 224, 243, 259, 262
resulted   81
resulting   57, 140
results 9, 35, 37, 54, 59, 67-68, 70, 73-74, 83, 132, 138-139, 163, 173, 178, 182, 186, 188, 191, 218, 237, 245, 249-250
retain 87, 97
retention   172
retrospect   122
return 53, 67, 89, 191
returns 189
revenue   25, 53
revenues   49
review 11-12, 115-116, 133, 145, 168, 180, 189, 211, 215, 226, 237, 257
reviewed   33, 131, 152
reviewers   236
reviews 11, 168, 178, 206, 210, 245
revised 60, 81, 156
revising 121
revisions   259
revisit 227
reward 50, 55, 59, 220
rewarded   20
rewards   80
rework 51
rights 1
rivals 114
routine 82, 156
routines   116
rubbish 229
running   107
rushing 198
safely 209
safety 85, 92, 214
Sampling   186
satisfied   103, 115, 180, 253, 262
satisfies 248
satisfying   21, 101
savings 39, 45-46, 51, 60

scenario 32
schedule 3-4, 29, 52, 72, 118, 139, 143-144, 147, 159, 168, 176-179, 185, 210, 224, 231-232, 245-246, 251
scheduled 160, 186, 196-197
schedules 167, 176, 213, 246
scheduling 160, 179, 192, 243
scheme 80
Science 174
scientific 174
Scorecard 2, 13-15
scorecards 80
Scores 15
scoring 11
scratch 122
screen 72, 93, 103
scripts 186
seamless 97
search 95
second 13
section 13, 25-26, 40, 55, 66, 76, 86, 129
sections 152
sector 247
secured 249
security 56, 85, 135, 186, 188-189, 225
seeing 128
segment 97, 108-109, 111, 123
segmented 33, 115
segments 28, 38, 107, 114, 125
select 86
selected 70, 140, 182
Selection 5, 212
selects 238
seller 180
sellers 1, 173
selling 83, 166, 226
-selling 245
senior 92, 100, 109, 123
sensitive 39, 138
sequence 162, 168
sequencing 143
series 12
serious 145

service 1-2, 7-8, 11, 23, 28, 42, 95, 97, 104, 108, 120, 151, 166, 184, 187, 212, 220-221
services 1, 8, 19, 50-51, 104, 111, 126, 136, 173, 213, 228-229, 234, 241, 251, 254, 257-259
setbacks 63
setting 95, 124, 245
several 8
severance 230
severely 65
shared 84, 146, 182, 227, 257
sharing 77, 131, 216
shorten 176
shorter 88
short-term 90, 244
should 7, 19, 34-35, 44, 46, 53, 70-71, 79, 82-83, 86, 89-90, 92, 94, 96-98, 102, 109, 112-113, 119, 121, 123-124, 131-132, 135, 137-140, 144-145, 156, 162-163, 170-171, 173-174, 185, 190, 193, 200, 202-205, 209, 212-213, 217, 232, 238, 257, 261
showing 139
signals 126
signatures 169
signed 151
signers 259
similar 30, 36, 56, 59, 68, 161, 163, 184, 198, 206
simple 96, 247
simply 9, 11, 227
simulator 236
single 129
single-use 7
situation 24, 41, 123, 180, 202-203, 206, 218, 247
skeptical 125
skills 22, 92-93, 165, 184, 194, 197, 235, 242-244, 263
slippage 207
smallest 21, 67
social 49, 125, 136, 208, 249
software 24, 144, 172, 180, 196, 200, 205, 215, 218, 251
solicit 32
soluiton 251
solution 65, 67-68, 70-73, 76-77, 151, 186, 251
solutions 67-73, 263
solving 236
Someone 7
something 140, 152, 184

source 5, 109, 118, 152, 181, 208, 212, 228
sources   56, 61, 76, 206, 233
special 37, 83, 133
specific   9, 21, 30, 37, 63, 112, 125, 128, 143-144, 153, 161, 163, 165, 169, 171, 176, 180, 184, 195, 197, 221, 224, 255, 257
specified   157, 159, 245, 257, 262
specify 235
Speech   147
spoken 117
sponsor   22, 140, 159, 253, 261
sponsored   30
sponsors   25, 197, 249
stability 54, 189
stable   249
staffed 29
staffing 80, 140
stages   178, 229
standard   7, 79, 82-83, 86, 169, 173, 189, 245, 251
standards   1, 11-12, 83, 85, 142-143, 153, 186, 188, 191, 215, 224, 245, 249
started 9, 165, 167
starting 12
stated   156-157, 159, 187, 195, 234, 255
statement   3, 12, 68, 133, 150, 181
statements   13, 26, 30-31, 40, 55, 60, 66, 76, 86, 129, 190
statistics   150
status   5-6, 61, 137, 160, 192, 202, 204, 220, 239, 247, 251, 264
steady 49
steering   142-143, 152
storage   229, 244
stories   34
straight 258
strategic   18, 24, 71, 73, 86, 91, 98, 114, 116, 142, 187
strategies   44, 105, 111, 118, 150, 153, 172, 177, 201, 214, 227
Strategy   1-6, 9-15, 17-19, 21-29, 31-55, 57-61, 63-66, 68-73, 75-76, 78-80, 82-93, 95-107, 109-111, 113-146, 148, 150-157, 159-163, 165, 167-184, 186-188, 190, 192-198, 200, 202-208, 210, 212, 214-216, 218-222, 224-226, 228, 231-233, 235, 237, 239, 241-243, 245, 247-249, 251, 253-257, 259, 261-265
Stream 96
strengths   103, 165, 254
stretch 124

strive 124
striving 133
strong 195
Strongly   12, 17, 27, 41, 56, 67, 77, 87
structural   235
structure   3-4, 72, 91, 96, 150, 154-155, 170, 176
structured   214
structures   243, 245
stupid 93
subdivided   157
subject 9-10, 30
submit 11, 223
submitted   11, 224
subsequent   159, 212
subset 21
sub-teams   235
succeed   58
success   20, 24, 28-29, 31, 36-37, 47, 53, 69, 75-76, 89-91, 98, 108, 116, 132, 142, 160, 167, 204, 210, 221, 227, 241, 261
successful   60, 76, 80, 88, 92-94, 126, 132, 138, 185, 220, 238, 241
succession   79
suffered   236
sufficient   139, 241-242
suggest   205, 222, 228
suggested   84, 224
suitable   49, 200, 231, 250
summarized   99
supervisor   195, 234, 237
supplier   123, 258
suppliers   28, 45-46, 64, 92, 105, 258
supplies   254
supply 49
support   7, 49, 66, 68, 79-80, 105, 109-110, 133, 147, 169, 195, 202, 217, 229, 246, 251, 264
supported   27, 58, 147
supporting   85, 125, 191, 197
supportive   194-195
supposed   99, 228
surface   84
SUSTAIN   2, 68, 87
sustaining   85, 136, 233
switching   45-46

symptom 17
system 11-12, 34, 92, 110, 133, 144, 147, 152, 156-157, 171, 192, 195, 200, 214, 225, 228, 230, 237, 241, 247-248
systematic 48, 50, 246
systems 48-49, 57, 59, 75, 80, 153, 229, 245, 247, 254
tactics 227
taking 53, 139, 221
talent 64, 100, 197
talents 93, 197
talked 22
talking 7
tangible 101, 249
target 39, 112, 122, 129, 139, 189, 238
targeted 101, 112
targets 124, 133, 180, 247
tasked 84
teaching 238
teamed 234
teaming 233
technical 71, 75, 139, 146, 206, 213, 238
techniques 65, 140, 173
technology 98, 108, 133, 166, 172-173, 202, 204, 233-234, 258
template 176
templates 7, 9
tender 257-258
tenders 257
tested 18, 73
testing 68, 70, 91, 187, 189, 249-250
thankful 8
themes 238
themselves 48
theory 78
things 74, 89, 120, 132, 181, 205, 210
thinking 63, 68, 100
thorough 185
thoroughly 151
thought 199
thoughts 44
threat 95, 122
threaten 176
threats 66
through 62, 65, 92, 101, 125, 206, 249
throughout 1, 168

throughput 172
tighter 125
time-bound 30
timeframe 182
timeline 224
timeliness 186
timely 39, 179, 192-193, 218, 222
timetable 168
Timing 198
todays 106
together 108, 234, 238
tolerances 70
tolerate 201
tolerated 161
tomorrow 85
topics 75
toward 80, 221
towards 65
traceable 192
traced 186
tracing 144
tracked 201
tracking 31, 86, 152, 176
traction 125
trademark 1
trademarks 1
trade-offs 196
trained 27, 32, 34, 186, 212, 215
training 22, 25, 39, 66, 80, 83-84, 216-217, 220, 228, 233, 238, 264
traits 108
Transfer 13, 26, 40, 55, 66, 76, 80, 84, 86, 129, 217, 252
transition 145, 205
translated 30
travel 233, 258
trends 57, 59, 63, 69, 100, 107, 140, 150, 187, 208
trigger 70
triggers 74
trophy 105
trouble 101, 104
trusted 94
trying 7, 24, 109, 116, 208
turning 90

typically 52
ultimate 113, 124
unable 234
unbiased 250
unclear 28
uncover 193
uncovered 146
underlying 75
undermine 109
understand 31, 132, 144, 172
understood 205, 243
undertake 203
undertaken 257
underway 69
uninformed 125
unique 96, 99, 106, 166, 233
uniquely 239
Unless 7
unpack 107
unresolved 169, 211
update 184, 261
updated 9-10, 61, 159, 168, 172
updates 10, 80, 251
upgrade 122
urgent 223
usable 193
useful 70, 77, 153-154, 264
usefully 12, 21
utility 102, 127, 175
utilizing 72
validate 247
validated 33, 35-36, 57, 131
Validation 247
validity 147, 242
valuable 7
values 92, 100, 123, 208
variable 106
variables 54, 59, 81, 226, 237
variance 6, 156, 192, 236, 245-246
variances 156, 178, 193, 210, 245
variation 17, 37, 42, 49, 52, 56, 61, 80
varieties 95, 120
variety 69

throughput 172
tighter 125
time-bound 30
timeframe 182
timeline 224
timeliness 186
timely 39, 179, 192-193, 218, 222
timetable 168
Timing 198
todays 106
together 108, 234, 238
tolerances 70
tolerate 201
tolerated 161
tomorrow 85
topics 75
toward 80, 221
towards 65
traceable 192
traced 186
tracing 144
tracked 201
tracking 31, 86, 152, 176
traction 125
trademark 1
trademarks 1
trade-offs 196
trained 27, 32, 34, 186, 212, 215
training 22, 25, 39, 66, 80, 83-84, 216-217, 220, 228, 233, 238, 264
traits 108
Transfer 13, 26, 40, 55, 66, 76, 80, 84, 86, 129, 217, 252
transition 145, 205
translated 30
travel 233, 258
trends 57, 59, 63, 69, 100, 107, 140, 150, 187, 208
trigger 70
triggers 74
trophy 105
trouble 101, 104
trusted 94
trying 7, 24, 109, 116, 208
turning 90

typically 52
ultimate 113, 124
unable 234
unbiased 250
unclear 28
uncover 193
uncovered 146
underlying 75
undermine 109
understand 31, 132, 144, 172
understood 205, 243
undertake 203
undertaken 257
underway 69
uninformed 125
unique 96, 99, 106, 166, 233
uniquely 239
Unless 7
unpack 107
unresolved 169, 211
update 184, 261
updated 9-10, 61, 159, 168, 172
updates 10, 80, 251
upgrade 122
urgent 223
usable 193
useful 70, 77, 153-154, 264
usefully 12, 21
utility 102, 127, 175
utilizing 72
validate 247
validated 33, 35-36, 57, 131
Validation 247
validity 147, 242
valuable 7
values 92, 100, 123, 208
variable 106
variables 54, 59, 81, 226, 237
variance 6, 156, 192, 236, 245-246
variances 156, 178, 193, 210, 245
variation 17, 37, 42, 49, 52, 56, 61, 80
varieties 95, 120
variety 69

various 178
vendor 131
vendors 21, 61, 142, 151
ventilated 229
verified 10, 33, 35-36, 57, 131, 173
verify 46, 48-50, 52, 54, 79-80, 82, 139, 150, 248, 260
verifying 43, 51-52, 258
Version 251, 266
versions 34, 38
versus 145
vertical 136
vested 112, 209
viable 113, 126, 155
viewpoint 261
viewpoints 261
violated 152
violations 153
virtual 91
vis-à-vis 205
vision 90, 92, 95, 140, 195
visualize 161
voices 135
volatility 200
waiting 112
warranty 1, 189
weaknesses 103, 136, 152, 212, 254
whether 7, 78, 121, 133, 257
widespread 128
willing 92, 97, 128, 206, 264
within 110, 157, 162-163, 174, 195, 208, 220, 224, 229, 237, 253, 258
without 1, 13, 45, 108, 224, 259
worked 73, 141, 198, 255, 263-264
workers 109, 172, 264
workflow 226-227
workforce 69, 92, 101
working 69, 78, 93, 110, 127, 137, 139, 194-195, 226
workload 90
Worksheet 4, 174, 182
writing 11, 149
written 1, 160, 229, 257
yesterday 18
yourself 95, 116, 127, 218

CPSIA information can be obtained
at www.ICGtesting.com
Printed in the USA
LVHW080213220719
624821LV00012B/229/P